EXPLORING WALES

W. T. BARBER

DAVID & CHARLES
Newton Abbot   London   North Pomfret (Vt)

British Library Cataloguing in Publication Data

Barber, W. T.
   Exploring Wales.
   1. Wales—Description and travel—1951-—Guide-books
   I. Title
   914.29′04′857   DA735
   ISBN 0-7153-8179-2

Typeset in Monophoto Plantin
by Latimer Trend & Company Ltd, Plymouth
and printed in Great Britain
by Redwood Burn Limited, Trowbridge, Wilts
for David & Charles (Publishers) Limited
Brunel House   Newton Abbot   Devon

Published in the United States of America
by David & Charles Inc
North Pomfret   Vermont 05053   USA

Contents

Acknowledgements

My thanks go to all who have helped in supplying me with special material which I have been able to use in this book. Very special thanks are due to my erudite friend, 'J.R.', a true Silurian and a good companion on my travels through Wales. His assiduous help in checking the printer's proofs have been invaluable. I am grateful for the careful editing of the manuscript by Mrs Jean Gay and for her suggestions for the insertion of additional material.

Author's Note

Specially prepared maps appear at the beginning of the chapters and, in most cases, they give a very clear indication of the route taken, and places of interest along the way.

If the reader requires more detailed information the Bartholomew's National Map Series: scale 1:100 000 is very useful:

No 11   Pembroke and Carmarthen
No 12   Cardiff and Glamorgan
No 13   Hereford and Gloucester
No 17   Aberystwyth and Cardigan
No 18   Vale of Severn and Radnor Forest
No 22   Mid-Wales
No 27   North Wales

The above clear easy-to-read maps of Wales have also now been published in book form by Hamlyn. The scale of 1·6 miles to 1 inch (1:100 000) enables the maps to be very detailed, and there is a most helpful index.

Historical Survey

It is not my intention here to provide a full history of Wales but rather to sketch in the background to what the reader will encounter in the journeys described in the main body of the book.

For many thousands of years men made little impression on the landscape of what is now Wales; their way of life—hunting and gathering food—meant that most of their traces were swallowed up in the primeval forest. This state of affairs only changed with the arrival of farming techniques in the Neolithic era (4000–2300 BC). Some of the forest was cleared, cattle rearing and crop growing began, and the scattered population became more attached to particular areas. A new way of life came into being yet, paradoxically, the most visible survivals from the period are the great collective graves the Neolithic communities built for their dead. These are the chambered long barrows (also known as megalithic tombs or cromlechs) which can fairly be described as our earliest surviving architecture. These structures consisted of a chamber—in which the remains and offerings were placed—built of large stone slabs, covered over by a long, rectangular barrow, or mound, of earth and rubble. Periodically, some of the tombs were reopened to accommodate further remains. The chamber stones could be very large: in the tomb at Tinkinswood, near Cardiff, the capstone—the horizontal roofing slab—weighs 40 tons. In some cases the original mound has been carried or eroded away, leaving the great stone skeleton exposed to view as at Pentre Ifan in the Preseli Hills. Much rarer were circular cairns with stone burial chambers but two examples may be seen in Anglesey at Bryn-Celli-Ddu and Barclodiad-y-Gawres.

Invaders from eastern and central Europe introduced the revolutionary metal-working skills of the Bronze Age (c2300–700 BC) Wales and again their graves provide some of the most obvious remains. By now the practice of collective burial had been superseded by single burials—without chambers—in round barrows or cairns of earth and boulders. These are the *tumuli* marked as such on Ordnance Survey maps; other words on the map such as *carn*, *garn* and *carnedd* also help to indicate their whereabouts. The rather mysterious standing stones (menhirs) and stone circles and rows were mostly erected at this time, although some date back to the late Neolithic era. The adjective 'mysterious' is used advisedly because their purpose is unclear and scholarly debate on their meaning continues to flourish. Perhaps the circles and rows were used by these

5

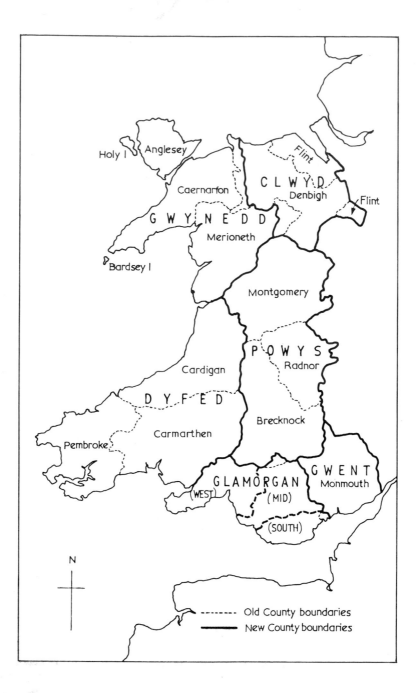

Holy I
Anglesey
Caernarfon
GWYNEDD
Merioneth
Bardsey I

Flint
CLWYD
Denbigh
Flint

Montgomery

POWYS
Radnor

Cardigan
DYFED

Carmarthen
Pembroke

Brecknock

GLAMORGAN
(WEST)
(MID)
(SOUTH)

GWENT
Monmouth

N

------ Old County boundaries
——— New County boundaries

early farmers as aids in measuring the movements of the moon and stars so that sowing, for example, could be regulated, while the single upright stones might have served as markers in cross-country journeys.

Towards the end of the Bronze Age there is evidence of increasing aggression and warfare, and defensive hilltop enclosures began to be built, especially in eastern Wales and the Marches; Dinorben in Clwyd and the Breidden hillfort in Powys are examples. However, it was the Celtic tribes of the succeeding Iron Age culture who made hillforts a permanent and conspicuous feature of the Welsh landscape.

The Celtic-speaking peoples came to the British Isles in two successive waves after about 500 BC. At roughly the same time the Celtic language divided into two branches, Brythonic (also Brittonic or British) and Goidelic. The Brythonic language gave rise, after many centuries, to Welsh, Cornish and Breton; similarly, Goidelic was the ancestor of Irish, Manx and Gaelic. These newcomers to Wales were warlike and warrior aristocracies, specialists in raiding warfare, dominated their tribes. Much of our knowledge of their domestic life is derived from the remains of their hillforts (since barrows had gone out of fashion). It is important to remember that many of them were not purely military in purpose but were rather defended farms and villages, the ramparts serving as a safeguard in times of danger. In religion the Celts' priests were the famous Druids, about whom little is truly known except that a cult of lakes and rivers was practised, and that Anglesey was an important centre for them.

Celtic Britain was fragmented into tribal areas and thus an easy target for the disciplined Roman armies which launched their first successful attack on the island in AD 43. The English lowlands were subdued by AD 47 but the tribes of western Britain, aided by a mountainous terrain, put up a more protracted resistance. However, by AD 80 all effective opposition to Roman power was at an end and for three-hundred years Wales became part of the province of Britannia.

The Romans, with their typical thoroughness, established legionary fortresses at Deva (Chester) and at Isca Silurum (Caerleon). From these two key bases roads ran west to marching camps at Segontium (Caernarfon) and Moridunum (Carmarthen); similar roads were built into the interior serving a network of smaller forts such as Cicutio (Brecon Gaer). Despite this, Wales never really became more than a frontier region for the Romans. Their culture only put down effective roots in the south-east and here the Celtic aristocracy grew to be at home speaking Latin; Venta Silurum (Caerwent) was the only sizeable town in Roman Wales and there were villas belonging to Romanised Britons along the southern coastal plain. Elsewhere, life for the Celtic tribes carried on much as before, on the conditions that order was kept and that

Rome got the manpower, corn and metals she wanted from the region.

By the late fourth century the established system was breaking down and western Britain began to appear as a source of easy pickings for Irish raiding parties (the Romans had never colonised Ireland); the Féni, from the central eastern coast of Ireland, were particularly troublesome in northern Wales. Following their standard practice of recruiting friendly barbarians as auxiliaries the Romans allocated the defence of this region to military colonists from the Votadini, a British tribe living between the Tyne and the Forth. By the early fifth century the settlers had effectively displaced the Féni from north-west Wales; the main memorial to these Irishmen is the county name of Gwynedd, their name in British form. The Votadini colonists, led by Cunedda and his sons Marianus, Romanus, Ceredig and Brychein, spread south and east to establish nearly all the royal dynasties of early medieval Wales. The names of some of the present districts of Wales can be easily traced to them: Meirionydd, Rhufoniog, Ceredigion and Brecknock.

The Romans abandoned the province in the early fifth century and in the following centuries the Britons waged a long struggle against Anglo-Saxon invaders. Wales was the only region where an independent British society survived and it is from this era onwards that we can properly refer to west-central Britain as Wales. It evolved on lines unique, with its own kings and laws, its own church and its own language and literature.

Although Christianity had been the Empire's official religion it really only took root in Wales during these early years of independence, the period known as the Age of the Saints. Missionaries from Gaul, fleeing the barbarian invasions, arrived in the western areas of the British Isles and found many converts among Celtic ruling families (St David himself was reputedly a great-great grandson of Cunedda). Thus it became a Christian duty, as well as a patriotic one, to resist the pagan Anglo-Saxons. With such influential backing the Word was carried throughout Wales by wandering holy men, trained in monasteries like Llanilltud Fawr in the Vale of Glamorgan. The activities of the founders of the Celtic Church are most clearly seen today in the names of places. Wherever they settled, an enclosure, or *llan*, was thrown up around their rough church; this term is now a Welsh word for 'church' and, linked to the name of the saint himself, occurs in many place names.

The Welsh language was in existence by the end of the sixth century, in those areas of the old Roman province where the Anglo-Saxons had not penetrated, and a superb epic poetry soon grew up to celebrate the deeds of this Heroic Age. The Welsh had traditionally called themselves the *Brython* (Britons) but this name was replaced by *y Cymry* (the compatriots) in recognition of their kinship with the British in other parts of the island, similarly struggling for survival; the English county name of

Cumbria is from the same root. The Saxons referred to the *Cymry* as *Wealeas* (Romanised foreigners), whence the 'Welsh' of modern English. By the mid seventh century the Welsh were separated from their fellow-countrymen in Cornwall, Cumbria and southern Scotland and in the eighth Offa of Mercia built his famous dyke, thereby establishing the frontier of Wales in approximately final form. Unfortunately, the mountainous core of Wales made it difficult to create a true political unity and the Welsh kingdoms often fought each other as much as the Saxons.

The Welsh, like the English, suffered from the depradations of the Vikings during the ninth and tenth centuries, but, while a certain amount of settling occurred the Welsh kingdoms preserved their independence. The assault on Wales began in earnest after the Norman Conquest of England in 1066. William I created some of his most powerful supporters the earls of Chester, Shrewsbury and Hereford, with the brief to pacify the Welsh. Following the river valleys the Normans took possession of eastern and southern Wales, the lowlands, in a remarkably short time but for two-hundred years thereafter political power see-sawed between the invaders and various independent princes. The areas which consistently offered the most resistance were in the mountainous north and west: Gwynedd, Clwyd, northern Powys and parts of Dyfed. Where the Normans held sway they quickly built castles of earth and timber (motte and bailey) at strategic points and introduced urban life to Wales by establishing new, walled towns at their feet, peopled by immigrants. Chepstow, Cardiff, Carmarthen, Pembroke and Tenby are examples. Later on, massive stone castles replaced the original structures, and these formed the centres of feudal lordships, virtually independent of the English crown. The old Celtic Church was absorbed into the mainstream of the Latin Church with the arrival of the Norman diocesan system and branches of the great continental religious houses. The latter, in particular the Cistercians, built many of the lovely abbeys, such as Tintern and Strata Florida, now so much part of the landscape.

From the middle of the twelfth century there was a Welsh political and cultural revival, a second Heroic Age. Able and efficient princes, like Owain Gwynedd in the north and Rhys ap Gruffyd in the south-west, harnessed Norman ideas on administration and warfare and successfully turned them on the enemy; they even built stone castles, as at Dolwyddelan near Blaenau Ffestiniog and the original Carreg Cennen near Llandeilo. This generation and their successors in the thirteenth century were concerned above all to rid Wales of the curse of political fragmentation, which had prevented the formation of a strong state, able to defeat a united England. Llywelyn the Great and Llywelyn the Last, both princes of Gwynedd, came very close to achieving complete control of Wales and in 1267 the second Llywelyn was recognised as Prince of

Wales by Henry III of England. However, Welsh national aspirations foundered on the rock of Edward I's determination to crush them for ever. In a campaign between 1277 and 1282 the English king destroyed all resistance to his rule in Wales. Llywelyn was killed in 1282 in a skirmish near Builth Wells and his brother Dafydd executed at Shrewsbury a little later. This marked the end of the Age of the Princes, an era which had begun in the time of Cunedda. Edward then built his chain of ten great castles to force the Welsh into permanent submission; they included Aberystwyth, Beaumaris, Caernarfon, Conway, Harlech and Rhuddlan. English-style shires were created in the north and the Marcher lordships controlled the rest of Wales.

The country remained politically quiet throughout the fourteenth century and then, in 1400, the Glyndwr revolt began. Owain Glyndwr, although descended from Welsh princes, was on the face of it a 'pillar of society', having spent seven years at the Inns of Court in London and fought for Richard II in Scotland. A personal quarrel with his neighbour, Reginald Grey, Lord of Ruthin, led him to attack Ruthin in September, 1400. The quarrel somehow became a movement of national liberation as more and more Welshmen joined him. Castles and towns, the hated symbols of foreign domination, were taken and destroyed, and by 1405 Glyndwr's forces controlled the whole of Wales. After his victories Glyndwr began to behave as the ruler of a sovereign state: parliaments were called at Machynlleth, Dolgellau and Harlech; plans were drawn up for two universities, one in the north and one in the south, and for the establishment of an archbishopric independent of Canterbury; the French government recognised him as the legitimate Prince of Wales. But the English fought back and by 1410 Glyndwr was on the run and in 1412 he simply disappeared, leaving behind a magical name and misery as the English gained revenge through a scorched-earth policy. Strict penal laws against the Welsh were to remain in force throughout the century.

In 1485 Henry Tudor (Harri Tudur) became Henry VII of England. His partly Welsh origins—his grandfather, Owen Tudor, had come from Penmynydd in Anglesey—caused great excitement amongst the Welsh and his victory at Bosworth was seen as their own, a successful end to the struggle of Arthur and Glyndwr. There is no doubt that the Tudors helped to advance the careers of many ambitious Welshmen but theirs was also the age when the framework of modern Wales was created, in which the differences between England and Wales were dimished. The two countries were united by Henry VIII and the English legal and administrative system introduced throughout Wales. The remaining Marcher lordships became shires and all shires and boroughs had representation at the parliament in Westminster. Furthermore, no holder of public office could use Welsh in the course of his duties; thus English became the language of advancement which led to a gradual division between the Welsh-speaking masses and the English-speaking gentry. However, the Welsh language received a tremendous fillip when Queen Elizabeth, concerned to convert Wales entirely to the Anglican Church, ordered that the Bible should be translated into Welsh; published in 1588 *y Beibl Cymreig* raised the standard of spoken and written Welsh, and ensured in religion at least that Welsh would not be superseded.

For two-hundred years Wales remained poor and traditional in comparison to England, with little commercial or urban development. In the Civil War, for example, it was basically loyal to the Stuart cause and one-hundred years after the Restoration life was apparently quiet and uneventful. The religious revival after this date, known as Methodism, took the authorities by surprise. Its causes are obscure but it was associated with the success of the circulating schools—founded by Gruffyd Jones to enable Welshmen to *read* their Bibles—and the effect of great preachers like Daniel Rowland and Hywel Harris touching the hearts and spirits of large numbers of people all over Wales. It led to another great divide which survived well into this century: the Anglican Church became identified with the gentry, England and Toryism, and the Chapel with ordinary Welsh people and radical politics.

At the same time as the religious revival we see the beginnings of industrialisation which by 1900 transformed the landscape in many areas and turned the Welsh into a predominantly urban people. In the south the first major industry was iron-smelting, to be followed after 1850 by steel making and large-scale coal mining; the latter so dominated the economy that it was nicknamed 'King Coal'. In the north there was a phenomenal expansion of the slate industry in the nineteenth century to meet both domestic and foreign demand. The effects of this revolution are with us today; suffice it to say that the physical remains of the earlier, superseded industries are now themselves the object of historical interest. Some will be visited on the journeys that now follow.

A tablet in Llanover, Gwent, is inscribed with this Welsh verse:

Pwy wyt, Ddfodwr?
Os cyfaill, gresaw calon i ti;
Os diether, lleteu garwch a'th erys;
Os gelyn, addfwynder a'th garchara.

Who art thou, comer?
If stranger, hospitality shall meet thee;
If enemy, courtesy shall imprison thee;
If friend, the welcome of the heart to thee.

Croeso i Gymru: Welcome to Wales.

W. T. Barber, 1982

11

I

Gwent and the Usk Valley

After subduing the eastern part of Britain, in AD 75 Julius Frontinus marched westwards to deal with the Silures. Where he crossed the Severn is uncertain; some say from Aust to Sudbrook in Gwent, where a base was established, but others claim it was at Gloucester. It is possible that the river was crossed in both places, as a means of dividing the Silurian forces.

The main road from Gloucester to Chepstow, the A48, follows the line of the old Roman way, and from Tutshill it curves down to the River Wye, where it crosses over from England into Wales. To a visitor crossing the Wye here for the first time the sight of Chepstow Castle on the very edge of a cliff high above the river is breathtaking. Here the Silures built their earthworks, and when the Romans came they topped them with a stronger fort, so when the Normans required a castle they could not ignore the possibilities of this cliff-top site. The present castle was begun in 1067 by William Fitz Osbern, created Earl of Hereford by William the Conqueror, and much of his work survives. The name of the town is derived from the Saxon 'chepe', meaning a market, and 'stowe', a town.

A castle tower, dating from the thirteenth century, served as a prison-home for twenty years for Henry Marten the regicide. It is now known as Marten's Tower. He was one of the judges who condemned King Charles I to death, suggesting that they . . . 'serve His Majesty as the English did his Scottish grandmother and cut off his head.' Marten was no respector of persons, for when Cromwell, in signing the king's death warrant, accidentally splashed ink on Marten he retaliated by causing his pen to splutter so that the ink flew into Cromwell's face.

Amid the town's mixture of well-proportioned Regency and Georgian buildings are several interesting inns, some of them associated with local trades and famous persons who have visited them. There is the Beaufort, the Lord Nelson and the Lord

Wellington. The Lord Nelson (now closed) with others were coaching inns. Most have interesting stories about the prominent people who stayed in them. George Borrow ended his tour of Wales (immortalised in *Wild Wales*) at a Chepstow inn in 1854, enjoying the wine and singing Welsh songs. His reckoning afterwards was 'something considerable'. Thackeray enjoyed the hospitality of the town and also the taste of Wye salmon.

Just south-west of the town is an important road junction where the A48 meets the A466, the tourist route from the M4 into the Wye Valley. Continuing downhill along the A48 to the foot of Pwllmeyric Hill the old Roman road goes on to the village of Caerwent, the Roman city of Venta Silurum. At the foot of Pwllmeyric Hill Welsh soldiers bearing the mortally wounded King Tewdric paused to rest. The Christian Tewdric had led them to defeat the pagan Saxons in battle at Tintern in AD 600, but he knew he was dying, so bade his men carry him to Mathern where they were to build a church in which he was to be entombed. When a new church became necessary his stone coffin was opened. Inside it were found the bones of the martyr-king with his skull bearing a scar where the saxon axe had struck him. Near the church is Mathern Palace where the Bishops of Llandaff in Glamorgan came to seek peace and rest in this quiet corner of Gwent, and across the fields is the gabled Tudor mansion of Moynes Court, believed to occupy the site of a castle of the de Knevils. It is now a private house and not open to the public.

Caerwent, a few miles away, is where the Romans set up their administrative headquarters for the area in about AD 75. This 'Market Town of the Silures' had its temples, basilica, bath-houses, wine shops and many fine villas. Enclosed by walls nearly 12ft thick and 15 to 20ft high this had been no mean city. Word soon got round about the luxury of the 'new town' and many of the Silures left their bleak hilltop settlements (such as that at Llanmelin Wood, one mile north-west of Caerwent) to sample the warmth (for the central heating was good) of this new civilisation. On the principle of 'if you can't beat them join them' the local people adopted Roman ways, and when the Romans left Britain many went with them; others returned to their camp in Llanmelin Wood. One visits Caerwent today because of the part it played in shaping the history of our land, and there is still a lot here to

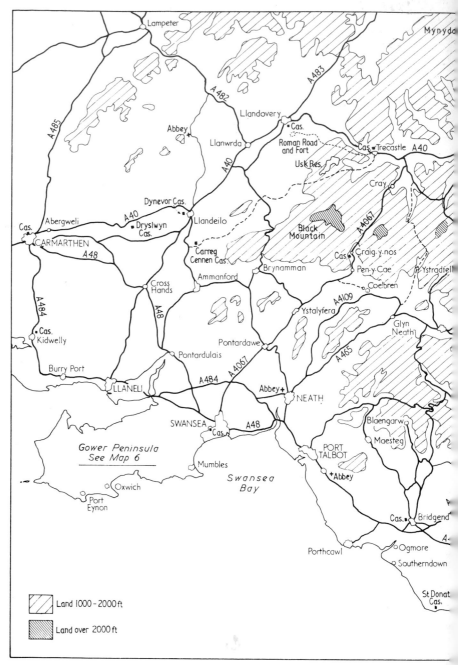

Map 1

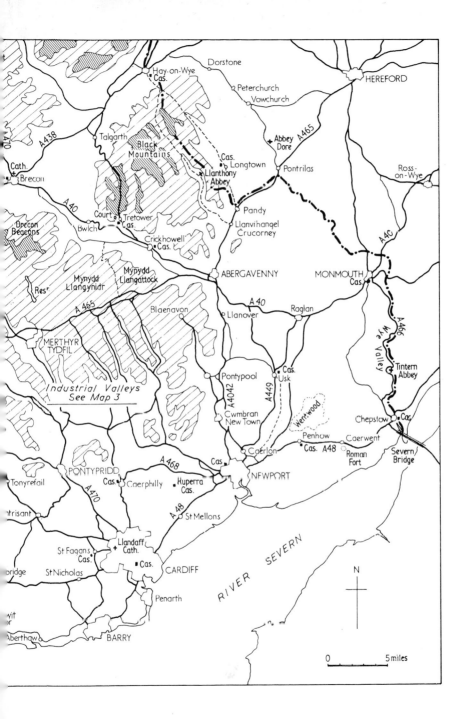

remind us of the past splendours of Venta Silurum, although most of the finds from the various excavations are in Newport Museum. Some relics can be seen inside the local thirteenth-century church.

The Roman engineers laid down roads which became convenient for others in later years; thus a tree-lined section of the A48 overlays one of their ways and leads to Penhow where stands Wales's oldest lived-in castle. In truth, it is more a fortified manor house than a castle and was built in the twelfth century to house retainers of the Earls of Hereford. For centuries it was neglected, its Great Hall used for storing grain, and when the moat became unnecessary it was filled in. The old castle has now been expertly restored so that it presents a fascinating picture of life from the twelfth to the nineteenth centuries. It was the first home in Britain of the famous Seymour (St Maur) family. The castle is not vast, but it was, and still is, a home—and probably the best surviving knight's castle along the Welsh border.

Chepstow Castle and the River Wye. Built on the site of earlier Silurian and Roman fortifications this Norman-built bastion guards the river crossing from England to south-east Wales

The Roman amphitheatre at Caerleon-on-Usk is the only one in Britain which
has so far been excavated. The earthen banks originally supported tiered seats for
6,000 spectators. Early Christians were probably martyred in this amphitheatre.
The photograph shows the north-west entrance to the arena.

About two miles away along the A48 is Llanbedr where a
modern sign saying 'Roman Road' directs you to a road which was
once a ridgeway along which the Romans marched to construct
their legionary fortress at Caerleon-on-Usk in AD 75. Caerleon was
the Roman Isca Silurum and, with York and Chester, the third
legionary fortress in Britain and the chief Roman base in South
Wales. An amphitheatre, large enough to have accommodated six
thousand people, and the foundations of a military barracks have
been uncovered—and even today fresh discoveries are being made
and recorded. There is a small museum in the village, but most of
the finds are in the National Museum in Cardiff.

The oval-shaped arena, surrounded by rising tiers of stone seats,
was built in AD 80 and excavated in 1926–7. How thrilled the
archaeologists must have been when they found a gladiator's
dagger lying in the centre of the arena, and a statue of the goddess
Diana near one of the eight entrances. Above one of these
entrances was the box where the Praetor and his favoured guests
sat, and on the opposite side of the arena is the gladiators' entrance.

17

You can still sit on the same stone seat used by them when waiting to entertain the noisy crowd. It is not difficult to imagine what took place there so many centuries ago.

It must have been a colourful scene with the eager crowds hurrying along the Broadway, anxious to arrive early so as to obtain the best possible seat. The Praetor, carried along in a canopied and gilded litter, resplendent in a white toga edged with a fretted design in imperial purple. Then the centurions, followed by the gladiators bearing their favourite weapons, the retarius with his net and trident, the laquarius with his lasso, and others carrying bossed and polished shields and short stabbing swords. The day's sport was inevitably brutal, and if the defeated gladiator had not fought well enough to please the bloodthirsty crowd and earn the chance to fight another day, their jeers on this Roman holiday made certain that the victor was given the 'thumbs down' sign by the Praetor to dispatch his unfortunate adversary.

There is a legend, first recorded in 1136 by Geoffrey of Monmouth in his *History of the Kings of Britain*, that King Arthur set up his Round Table in the centre of the deserted amphitheatre when he made Caerleon one of his capitals. This legend must have been accepted by the poet Tennyson, for he stayed at the riverside Hanbury Arms to gather material for his *Idylls of the King*.

The Romans continued to force their way into Wales, following the river to the town of Usk, a place which they called Burrium, although the original site has not been located. The ancient road to Usk has always been accepted as being of Roman origin, running between the river and the wooded slopes of Wentwood on which they built a chain of outposts.

Burrium was fortified a long time before the Romans came to Britain. When the Norman de Clares came they built a fortress on a high cliff above the centre of the little town. Soon after its completion the Norman masons were sent 'an arrow flight away' to build a priory, said to have been a retreat for ladies of noble birth, and for those seeking solace after a broken romance. Not all of the ladies were able to forget the joy of their former secular life for, in 1401, Adam of Usk, a priest and chronicler, suggested that the prioress had an adulterous affair with John Fitz Piers, senschal of the castle. The priory gatehouse still stands and part of the main building has been converted into a comfortable home.

Leave Usk at the sign of The Three Salmons, on the corner of the road to Llanvihangel Gobion, and after crossing the river at Chain Bridge, and again at Pant-y-Goitre, the Romans' next keypoint at Abergavenny (Gobannium) is along the main road from Raglan and Monmouth. To the Romans, Abergavenny was an important centre from which they could advance to establish bases in what is now the southern part of the county of Powys before pushing their way into western Wales. Just beyond the riverside town of Crickhowell they established a fort at Pen-y-Gaer from where they were able to drive the Silures back through a *bwlch* (pass) into an open area where they could more easily contain them, and, as the ravine was narrow where the village of Bwlch now stands, a broad frontal attack from their enemies was not possible. In this area the old Ordnance Survey map (Sheet 141)

The Vale of Usk. On its long journey from the bleak moorlands of Fforest Fawr, the Usk approaches the village of Talybont (*Wales Tourist Board*)

indicates the line of several stretches of the old Roman road. One, a subsidiary road, starts from Talybont to climb a hillside to another of their forts at Dol-y-Gaer overlooking the Talybont valley.

After securing the *bwlch* the route to Brecon was much safer, which was a very important point for the control of the Usk valley and the southern foothills of the Epynt mountains. Precisely north-east of Brecon the Romans first of all attacked and secured the Celtic earthworks of Pen-y-crug, making good use of this ready-made fort until it was possible for them to build a more permanent one for their soldiers; they eventually built Cicutio (Y Gaer) at the confluence of the Usk and Yscir rivers. There are still ample remains of the stone walls, watchtowers and guardhouses of a fort which must have been luxurious after the primitive ditches and earthen walls of the Silures. Both fortifications can be easily reached from the B4520 road out of Brecon.

Not far along the A40 to the west is Trecastle. After passing the Castle inn in that village a turning on the left leads to the end of our Roman way and the fort of Y Pigwn. This turning soon joins an unmistakable Roman-engineered marching way across the bleak and lonely moors of Mynydd-bach Trecastle, an upland route between the *cwms* of Wysg and Dwr. If it is the late afternoon of a bright day the sun will have sunk low enough to gild the waters of the Usk Reservoir in Cwm Wysg, and beyond the Black Mountain of east Dyfed will have cast deep shadows over the moors.

Roman roads played a big part in the subjugation of the land and its people, the proud inhabitants of a savage land. These military roads were built to last, and here and there it is still possible to appreciate the lasting quality of the Roman construction. Time and climatic erosion make part of the road difficult to follow, but a good map will indicate its course. Two small stone circles, of even greater age than the fort of Y Pigwn, stand near the fort. Mounds of earth and fallen stones are all that remain of the moorland outpost, but the general outline of the two rectangular enclosures, one within the other, can still be traced.

The Black Mountain rises from the moorlands at the western end of the Brecon Beacons National Park, its high ridges separating West Glamorgan from Dyfed and Powys. Below the north slopes of the mountain are the twin lakes of Llyn-y-fan-fach and Llyn-y-fan-fawr. At the foot of Bannau Sir Gaer is the larger of the two lakes, Llyn-y-fan-fawr, a mysterious pool with a strange legend.

An ancient story tells of how a young farmer saw three beautiful girls rise out of the lake and walk towards him through the mist. He fell in love with one of them at first sight. They promised that if on the following morning he could pick her out—and as they were so much alike this was difficult—the maiden he fancied would become his wife. By some clever subterfuge he was able to choose the right one, so she married him and brought with her a dowry of many fine cattle. The young farmer was very happy with his fairy-wife, and four fine sons were born to them. One day, however, his wife being slow in fetching something he required, he tapped her on the shoulder three times, saying: 'Go, go, go!' No self-respecting fairy could suffer this treatment from a mere mortal, so she returned to the lake and vanished, leaving her unhappy husband to wander the shores of the lonely lake, brooding and weeping for his lost love.

The Usk is born at the feet of these Carmarthen Fans, flowing through the open moorland until it becomes wide enough to require a ford on the mountain road from Trecastle into the beautiful and historic former county of Breconshire. At the ford a signpost marks the boundary between Breconshire and Carmarthenshire (now Powys and Dyfed), and the river, now well-formed, flows northwards to feed the Cwm Wysg Reservoir, then alongside the mountain road to Trecastle, a village of stone-roofed houses overlooked by the mound of a vanished Norman castle.

The medieval town of Brecon is about ten miles away, and here the towers of another Norman castle and cathedral overlook the old bridge across the Usk. It is said that the castle, which belonged to William the Conqueror's half-brother, was largely built with stones taken from a nearby Roman fort, so perhaps some of the stonework of the adjoining Castle Hotel was originally tooled by Roman craftsmen. The Welsh name for Brecon is Aberhonddu, a softer and more musical-sounding name. Apart from its fine cathedral dating from the thirteenth and fourteenth centuries the town has several other interesting buildings. In the High Street at No 47 is where the famous actress Sarah Kemble was born, and in Ship Street is another building reputed to have once belonged to the family of Anne Boleyn. Then there is the Deanery where King

Charles I slept in 1645, and hospitality was also offered here to Sir Charles Price who translated the Bible into Welsh. The town has a small museum containing many interesting relics of prehistoric and Roman times.

Road, river and canal run side by side out of Brecon. The canal, the Brecon & Abergavenny (sometimes known as the Monmouthshire & Brecon), crosses the Usk in a stone aqueduct at Llanfrynach. Soon the notch of the *bwlch* is seen ahead, near the place of the same name. Here, Owain Glyndwr and his men once had to force their way through against a hail of English arrows. At the foot of the long curving road down from the *bwlch* a lane on the right leads to one of the most beautiful stretches of the Usk at Llangynidr Bridge. On a high knoll above the river is Gliffaes Guest House, a beautiful house built in an Italian style, surrounded by fine gardens with rare trees and, in season, masses of colourful rhododendrons.

Further downriver is Crickhowell, a town which suffered fire and slaughter at the hands of Norman and Welsh. The town is named after the *crug* (fort) of Hywel which stands on a mountain overlooking its narrow streets. Hywel-ap-Rhys, known as Hywel Dda (Hywel the Good), was a tenth-century king of southern Wales who laid down strict laws for the guidance of the people, but it is not known if he, like Moses, came down from the mountain with his commands inscribed on tablets of rock. Look for the sign of the Bear in the main street; it is almost a pictorial guide to the town and district, and hangs over cobbled paving outside an old coaching inn. On the sign is painted a great brown bear equipped with rod and fishing tackle. He holds in his paw a large salmon and behind him the artist has painted the *crug* of Hywel.

From the outskirts of the town a mile-long straight road goes to Llangrwyne. On a wet night about ten years ago a car travelling at high speed along this stretch of road crashed into the end stonework of the bridge over the Grwyne Fawr. The occupants of the car, which caught fire, were burned to death. One of them was a well-known singer of popular songs named Dickie Valentine. Morbid people still refer to the bridge as 'Valentine's Bridge'. The water flowing under this unhappy bridge today is crystal-clear, but once it brought Norman blood into the Usk. On that day the Norman, Richard de Clare, his son and retainers rode through a wooded pass on their way to Abergavenny Castle. This was a splendid opportunity for the Welsh chieftain Morgan-ap-Owen to pay off old scores; he ambushed the Normans, making sure that not one escaped with his life. Even today, the place where they were slain is known as Coed-y-Dias: 'The Wood of Vengeance'.

On a mound above the river at Abergavenny stands the most notorious of Norman fortresses. It was to this castle in 1175 that William de Braose, Lord of Abergavenny, invited Sitsyllt ap Dafnawld and seventy of his followers to a feast in celebration of a Christmas truce. According to custom they laid down their arms before sitting down at their host's table. The sight of rich foods, wine and mead amazed the Welshmen. This was indeed a celebration, but what a bloody one it turned out to be. The treacherous de Braose had made plans, and at a pre-arranged signal his armed soldiers rushed into the hall to transform the jovial scene into one of bloody slaughter, cutting and hacking until the massacre was complete. The historian Camden considered de Braose as 'the ogre of all Lord Marchers, the bloodiest of a grim breed'.

Abergavenny was once the place to come for the best Welsh flannel, but when customers found that the innermost folds of weaves were of lesser quality than the outer this trade declined. When wigs were fashionable those made and sold at Abergavenny were highly regarded. At one time the town and surrounding district was also reputed to be an ideal place for the cure of tuberculosis, so long as the patient drunk plenty of goats' whey. The history of the town goes back to Roman times, and in the Priory Church of St Mary the effigies and alabaster tombs of the lords and ladies of Abergavenny reflect the story of medieval times and later years.

A few miles south of the town a road, the A471, crosses the Usk at Pant-y-Goitre Bridge where it is often possible to see the salmon basking in the shallows. From here to the town of Usk is one of the finest stretches of the river for taking succulent salmon. Tales of romance and history connected with the river are far more credible than the tales told by its fishermen. On top of Clytha Hill the ramparts and ditches of an ancient fort were defended by the brave Silures of Gwent in a fierce battle against the Romans. A wood crowning the ancient earthworks is still called 'The Wood of Spears'. Trostrey and Estervarney are two place-names connected with more recent history. Across the river at Estervarney a forge was worked by the monks of Tintern Abbey in the Wye Valley, and from Trostrey iron from an old forge was sent south down river to Newbridge-on-Usk to be shipped from there to Newport.

The grey towers of another Norman castle overlook the river and the town of Usk. Richard II used this castle as a royal residence, finding good sport in fishing the river for trout and salmon. Some historians have claimed that Edward IV and Richard III were born at the castle, but Richard, of course, was born at Fotheringay. From the town square a road follows the river through Llantrisant to Newbridge-on-Usk where on a hilltop is a church containing a reminder of the Roman occupation. It is a memorial stone to:

JULIUS JULIANUS, SOLDIER OF THE SECOND AUGUSTAN LEGION, OF 18 YEARS SERVICE AND 40 YEARS OF AGE, HAS BEEN BURIED HERE AT THE CHARGE OF HIS BELOVED WIFE.

This unusual memorial stone was found during excavations in the churchyard.

Between Newbridge and Caerleon the narrow road runs alongside the A449 until deviating to follow the Usk to Caerleon where a battered grey tower guards the river crossing and the entrance to the 'City of the Roman Legions'. At Newport, three miles away, the last riverside castle is sighted and the Usk is crossed for the last time. The journey from its source ends at the gates of a great dock, through which pass ships from all parts of the world. Here is the mouth of the river, its tidal flow now merging with the waters of the Bristol Channel.

A canal once ran between Newport and Brecon, a considerable part of which it is still possible to discover on foot or by boat. Designed in the late eighteenth century to carry stone, coal and iron from the producing areas to the coast, it originally consisted of two separate canals (the Brecon & Abergavenny and the Monmouthshire), but in 1812 they were linked by a junction at Pontymoile, creating a through route, and in 1865 the Monmouthshire Canal Company bought the Brecon & Abergavenny outright. However, the Monmouthshire is now derelict while the B&A, some thirty miles long, has been restored. It passes through some of the most beautiful scenery in Britain.

A good place to start exploring this canal is Mamhilad, a few miles north of Pontypool. From there the towpath can be walked to Llanover where an old mill, now converted into an attractive dwelling, once supplied grain to load the barges coming from Llanfoist Wharf near Abergavenny. The latter place also received the ore and limestone brought down the steep incline from workings on the Blorenge and Coity mountains. This activity is vividly described by Alexander Cordell in his book *Rape of the Fair Country*. Nature has formed a great hollow in the side of the Blorenge above Llanfoist, a natural arena where the strong champions from the steel and mining villages came to slog it out in bare-fist combat, man to man, toe to toe and with no time limit.

From Llanfoist the canal flows through the Usk valley to Gilwern and Govilon, two places where it is possible to hire canal boats. On the mountain above, prominent against the skyline, is the 'Lonely Shepherd', turned to stone so that he might more easily endure the wear of wind and rain as he guards the sheep on a

One of the characteristics of the Brecon & Abergavenny Canal, built between 1797 and 1812, was the numerous horse-drawn waggon-ways that connected it to quarries and mines. Lying entirely within the Brecon Beacons National Park, it now provides an idyllic route through some of the finest scenery in Wales

mountain ridge above Pen-yr-heol. According to a local legend, and some folk swear it is true, the limestone monolith was once a local farmer whose wife, because of his insistent cruelty, drowned herself in a nearby pool. For his cruelty the farmer was turned to stone and, so the story goes, he wanders the mountainside on Midsummer Night searching for his lost wife, returning at dawn to continue his long and lonely vigil.

Below the standing stone a track follows the base of an escarpment beneath Llangattock moors. In the vertical face of the limestone escarpment small entrances give access to cold dank passages running for many miles under the moors. An old Sunday School at the foot of the escarpment serves as a meeting and storage place for the hardy people who come here to make a tortuous, belly-crawling way into the mysterious world beneath Llangattock Mountain. These small openings lead to a beautiful underworld and one of the most extensive cave systems in Britain. The Brecon Beacons National Park Information Sheet No 3 lists and locates all caves and the clubs which explore them.

In 1839 Chartist leaders and their supporters hid inside the caves to avoid arrest and deportation. Determined to prepare and organise for a final assault on Newport they brought with them weapons captured or stolen from the militia, and also tools to fashion additional weapons of steel and iron. In the depths of the caves they sweated from the fierce heat of improvised furnaces as they laboured to shape the liquid metal into swords, pikes and spears. It must have been an eerie scene with the lanterns projecting enlarged and distorted shadows along the uneven walls of the cave, the hammer blows of the smiths echoing a rhythmic cadence from the rock walls of underground chamber and passage.

When they were ready they started to march south. It was raining heavily, but as they reached the outskirts of Newport the sun shone brightly, so perhaps they considered this to be a good omen. But the soldiers of the Crown were better prepared and armed, so as the rebels turned from Stow Hill into Westgate Square devastating volleys of musket fire poured into them. In wild confusion the untrained men were unable to reform, so dropping their improvised weapons they fled. After a long and bitter struggle the Chartists had lost the day. However, their revolt brought about changes which were of benefit to all.

26

Many inns were built on profitable sites alongside the canals. The Coach and Horses inn at Cwm Crawnon must have been a favourite place for the thirsty bargees to refresh themselves before taking their heavy craft through the low dark tunnel at Talybont. The towing horses were unshackled and led over the top of the tunnel, then the bargees, lying on their backs, 'walked' the roof of the tunnel. The scuffed and shiny stonework of the arch proves that this was the method used to take the barges through. Many of the inn's older customers remember the time when barges passed the bar window on their way to Brecon or Newport, and of funny incidents such as the time when Twm, or Dai, forgetting to lower his head as the barge entered the tunnel was knocked into the canal. And there are strange stories of local happenings and traditions, one being of a plant or herb found on the mountain above the canal, but only where Danish blood has been split. It is called Llyieyn Gwaed Gwye, 'The Herb of the Blood Man'. (Danish blood had been spilt in this area when the Usk valley was raided by them in AD 893.)

Just before reaching the canalside village of Talybont a narrow lane goes over a canal bridge up to a high ridge between Dyffryn Crawnon and the Talybont valley. It soon becomes a track along an open area sloping away from both sides of a ridge just beyond Tor-y-Foel mountain. The rough rutted ridgeway track is marked on the map as a 'Roman Road', ending about two miles away at their mountain encampment of Dol-y-Gaer.

Just beyond Talybont village is Llanhamlach and the last canal lock before reaching Brecon. After crossing the Usk by a stone aqueduct the canal runs alongside the main road into Brecon. Now narrow and reduced to an insignificant stream it trickles between the towpath and a yard to expire with a quiet gurgle under the ancient streets of Brecon.

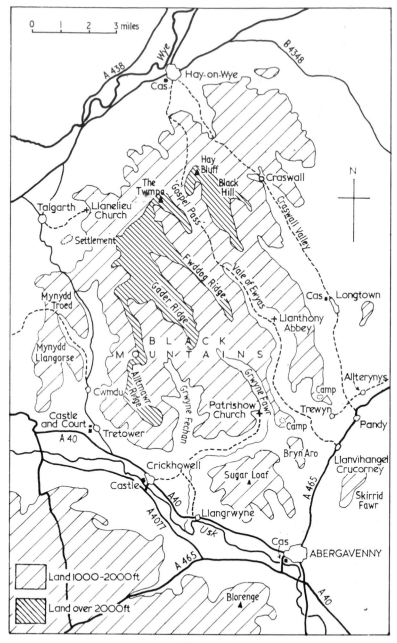

Map 2

2

The Black Mountains
and the Industrial Valleys

The Black Mountains belong to Gwent, Powys and western Hereford and Worcester. The geography of the region offers alternative ways of exploration. All the mountain ridges are easily reached from the lowlands, but if the tourist feels that he is unable to walk the ridges a tour by car round the perimeter of the mountains can be very satisfying. The first part of this chapter describes such a tour.

The journey starts from Abergavenny by taking the main Brecon road to the village of Llangrwyne, a few miles away; from there a lane curves its way into the Grwyne valley and, like most lanes in the Black Mountains, it twists its way through *cwms* which are winding and steep. Above the valley, on a small plateau carved out of the hillside, stands the lonely church of Partrishow. Its very isolation has saved it from the despoiler; this is fortunate, for inside is one of the most beautiful examples of the woodcarver's art to be found in Britain.

The very simplicity of the church interior accentuates the beauty of the rood screen and loft. With its delicately carved and cusped panels there is nothing brash, and the Irish oak has been left in its natural colour. The church is dedicated to St Issui, the hermit priest who built the first cell here on the banks of Nant Mair or St Mary's Brook. Nearby was a well with curative powers where, after drinking from it, a wealthy eleventh-century traveller was cured of leprosy. In gratitude he financed the building of a new church.

During the Dark Ages symbolic and highly coloured wall paintings were often used to persuade, and sometimes frighten, the illiterate into a state of piety and respect for holy scripture. In comparison with the beauty of the screen the wall painting here is ugly and brutal: 'Time' is shown as a skeleton carrying a scythe, spade and hour-glass, quite obscene in such a peaceful place. It has been said that many attempts have been made to wash the 'Red Devil' away but 'it always returns because it is painted in blood!'

Just outside Llangrwyne a tall standing stone guards the entrance to a military camp. This stone, and another about half a mile away, may have been set up by rival chieftains as mark-stones along their tribal boundaries—for blood was apt to be shed if anyone 'over-stepped the mark', and a large vertical stone was an obvious one.

Crickhowell's castle mound and ruined Norman tower are surrounded by a pleasant park and playground for local children, but in this area there are many cairns and mounds marking sites of less peaceful use. Just outside the town, between the main road and the River Usk, are several prehistoric mounds and the remains of a burial chamber dating from 2000 BC.

Tretower Court is a perfect example of a late medieval period home built around a courtyard with a curtain wall and gatehouse. Henry Vaughan, the Welsh poet and patriot, lived here in the seventeenth century

Glanusk Park, a mile west of Crickhowell, marks the point where the A479 turns off the Brecon highway and climbs through a valley to Talgarth. A short way along this road is Tretower Castle standing behind a medieval manor house. The first castle on this site was of the usual palisade on a bank above a ditch. When the Normans captured it from its Welsh owner Bleddin they built a stronger fortress in the shape of a huge square hall-keep. In later years they strengthened it by surrounding it with a circular tower. But even this form of double indemnity was not able to withstand Glyndwr who left it in ruins. After dealing with the castle Glyndwr turned his attentions to the manor house, Tretower Court, so at the end of the fifteenth century it was necessary to repair and improve it. Even so, Tretower Court is considered to be one of the finest examples of a medieval home in Wales. For generations it was the home of the Vaughan family, whose best-known representative is the poet Henry Vaughan (1622–95). Indeed, he loved the region so much that he was known as the 'Silurist' after the Silures, the ancient inhabitants of the area.

Following the Rhiangoll stream the road through the valley becomes narrower after Cwmdu is reached. With secret *cwms* cutting into the hills on either side it must have been an easy place for a sudden ambush and a quick retirement, so that an army marching through this dark valley would have been under constant fear of attack. The highest point of the road is reached at the pass of Pen-y-genfford. From a rutted lane it is possible to climb up to the earth ramparts of Castell Dinas, a place not intended to be a scenic viewpoint but a fortress that could be easily defended. These uplands between Usk and Wye have a long history of fighting and feuding, treason and treachery; so one twelfth-century writer was correct when he wrote:

> Brecknock is full of treason and there is war in Ystrad Towy.
> In Ewyas is found hatred and starvation,
> In Glyn Bwlch are mangling and sharp words,
> In Talgarth robbery and shame, bribery and lawyers.

Further along the road are the earthworks of an ancient settlement, but unlike Castell Dinas this was a place of civilian habitation, large enough to contain many huts and stockades for cattle. Partly enclosed by a stream and in good pasture and grazing land, the site was ideal. The people who lived there also had places of worship and sepulture, for the district around Talgarth has more than a fair share of stone circles, tumuli and cromlechs.

Welsh chieftains and other famous people lived in and near Talgarth. One, who saved the life of his king at Agincourt, was Sir Roger Vaughan who lived a mile away at Porthamal. His house was larger than it is today, with a strong tower pierced with archers' loopholes and other defensive features to deter the invader. Nearby this house is another interesting home, Gwernyfed Hall, where lions, adorned with oak leaves and acorns, are set on top of the entrance piers of the drive. The house contains a dining table and chair once used by King Charles I. Years ago it also had a macabre relic connected with the unfortunate monarch: a wooden snuff box reputed to have been made from a piece of the block used at his execution.

The steep escarpment of the Black Mountains shadows the small hamlet of Llanelieu, a name as difficult to pronounce as it is to spell. If you say 'Llan-elyoo' this would be approved by most Welsh-speaking natives, although some people might have difficulty with the 'Llan'. To help him achieve correct pro-nunciation there is a story that a bishop was once instructed to 'lift your lordly tongue to the roof of your episcopal mouth and hiss like a gander'. So this oralistic trick, followed by 'elyoo', sufficed. Llanelieu church has an interesting fifteenth-century rood screen and loft, but compared to the one at Partrishow it is crude and home-spun, its only decorative feature being the red and white roses stencilled in random pattern on the rough planking of loft and tympanum. Wishing to prove their impartiality during the Wars of the Roses the local parishioners thought it wiser, and safer, to display the emblems of York *and* Lancaster.

To complete a journey by car round the perimeter of the Black Mountains it is necessary to drive on to Hay-on-Wye which is about five miles away. The road runs on the Welsh side of the Wye, but to complete the circuit one crosses the border from Powys into Hereford and Worcester. However, who can say that he has never been tempted by the fruit in a neighbour's garden? In any case this part of England was once a part of Wales.

Now, if reference is made to the map (I recommend Bartholomew's map 13—National Series 1:100 000), a 'Golden

Valley' is entered, running alongside and close to the eastern flank of the Black Mountains. At the head of the valley is Dorstone where the Devil visits the local church at New Year to read out the names of those doomed to die during the next twelve months. Another lurid story is connected with a spot just north of Dorstone; it is marked on the above map as Scotland Bank, owing its name to the story that some wild Highlanders fleeing from the Battle of Worcester in 1651 were ambushed by even wilder Welshmen. It is said that a brook near the encounter 'ran red with blood for three days'.

Further down the valley are the villages of Vowchurch and Turnastone, owing their names, according to a local story, to the fact that a lady *vowed* that she would build her *church* before another lady (her sister) could *turn a stone*. Beyond these two villages the valley opens out to pleasant pastureland where the foundations of Abbey Dore, the 'Golden Abbey', were laid down in the twelfth century by Robert, the Norman lord of Ewyas who, perhaps not unselfishly, offered the building to the Cistercian monks who were very skilled in farming and care of the land. Here was a site very much to their liking.

Soon the main trunk road from Abergavenny to Hereford is reached, and the border is crossed back into Gwent and Wales. Close to our route can be found three Marcher castles—Grosmont, Skenfrith and the White Castle, collectively known as the Three Castles. Throughout the Middle Ages they were held in common ownership, controlling the area between Abergavenny and Monmouth, between the Black Mountains and the Wye. Grosmont is situated on the B4347, ten miles north-west of Monmouth; Skenfrith is on the B4521, eleven miles north-east of Abergavenny; and White Castle is located off the B4233 at Llantilio Crossenny, seven miles east of Abergavenny. Before reaching Abergavenny, the starting point of this Black Mountains journey, stop for refreshment at Llanvihangel Crucorney where you will find the oldest inn in Wales, and it claims to be the second oldest in Britain.

The foundations of the Skirrid Mountain Inn were laid down less than half a century after the Norman Conquest. The inn has been used as a Court of Justice, and many interesting features of those days can still be seen. One is the square-welled staircase which, as well as giving access to the upper floors, had a sinister as well as functional reason for its design. Halfway up the stairs a small room (now used as a ladies' room) once served as a cell where prisoners spent their last night after being sentenced to death. This small mezzanine room was a halfway stop for the unfortunate being soon to commence his journey to Heaven or Hades—for it was but a short way up to the improvised gallows beam above the stair-well. At the bottom of the staircase is the slab on which the bodies were placed after execution. It is recorded that the last person to be hanged at the ancient inn was tried and sentenced by Judge Jeffries, the notorious 'Hanging Judge'. The man was hanged for sheep-stealing, a crime then considered more serious than murder. Strange noises have been heard and ghosts are said to haunt the small room halfway up the stairs; one is said to be the spirit of a one-eyed felon who cheated the hangman by stabbing himself to death. Satan, or a particularly mischievous poltergeist, makes a nightly call and, to placate this uninvited guest, a pewter mug topped with the best brew is placed on a shelf in the main bar every night before the landlord and staff retire to bed.

To appreciate the full beauty of this mountainous area one should walk at least one of the ridges, particularly when the mountain slopes are covered with bluebells. Pandy on the main Abergavenny to Hereford road is a good starting point.

Two interesting old houses stand in the shadow of the Hatterall mountains. One is the small mansion of Allterynys, once the home of the Cecils who descended from the family of Sytsyllt. One of them became Lord Burleigh, a favourite minister of Queen Elizabeth I. It is probable that the Welsh origin of the Cecils, and the Herberts, helped them find favour with the Tudors. A mile away is Trewyn, an elegant chateau-like mansion. Inside are spacious rooms with deeply moulded woodwork and decorative plaster ceilings with ornate cornices. On the walls are paintings of famous soldiers, administrators and other ancestors of the owner of this lovely house.

Behind Trewyn a track climbs the mountain to an Iron Age fort. From the ramparts the land, close-contoured, tumbles down into a valley until it flattens to form the plainland of south Hereford and Worcester. Across the Vale of Ewyas (Llanthony Valley) another track climbs up to the Fwddog Ridge and another ancient hill fort at Twyn-y-Gaer. These two forts command the entry to the Vale of Ewyas, a valley, according to Giraldus, 'about an arrow-shot broad'.

On the right of the Hatterall ridgeway is the Craswall Valley with Longtown, an interesting village with a ruined Norman castle and many picturesque old houses. Longtown lies between the castle and Mynydd Merddyn where, according to legend, the wizard Merlin is buried. Merlin, like King Arthur, has caves, stones and burial places in all parts of Wales, so Mynydd Merddyn is as likely a place for him to have been buried as any other. With its long straggling street Longtown is aptly named, and the Normans considered its position between two rivers a good place to build a castle.

The cliffs of Black Daren are ahead, and soon the ridgeway widens to form a plateau. Here the colour of the rock changes from black to red, but black must be the favourite colour here, for there is Little Blackhill Farm, Great Blackhill Farm and straight ahead is the black precipice of Blackhill Mountain. This mountain is also called Cat's Back, so it is a certain bet that it was a reference to a *black* cat.

The ridgeway is wild and there is a feeling of remoteness. In bad weather one could easily get lost, so it must be hoped that the eerie story of the friendly spectral guide is a true one, and that the story of the 'Old Lady of the Black Mountains' who proves to be a false guide is untrue. These legends—good or bad—can be ignored, for it is a rare day if you do not meet some healthy-complexioned youngsters or pony-trekkers walking or hoofing their way along the mountain tracks.

The ridgeway ends at Hay Bluff, and if it is late afternoon the low sun sharpens the contours of the hills. White sheep will be seen grazing on the lower slopes of the Bluff, and on the plateau below wild ponies gallop through the heather. To the west, honey-tinted from the diffused light of the late sun, is the steep northern escarpment of the Black Mountains.

Bwlch-yr-Efengel, between Hay Bluff and the Twmpa, is at times a wild and uninviting place. According to legend St Peter, who had withstood many storms, stood here with his brother apostle Paul. It was a cold, grey day and St Peter decided that he had suffered enough of these wild Welsh mountains, so he climbed

35

over the Bluff to seek a less boisterous spot where he could found a church. He came to a golden valley in Herefordshire and so gave his name to Peterchurch. As their mission in this part of Wales was to convert the heathen, Peter and Paul named this wild gap in the mountains Bwlch-yr-Efengel (the Pass of the Evangelist) or as it is called today, 'Gospel Pass'.

Pony tracks going down the flank of the Bluff lead to the lowlands, so it is better to cross the pass and proceed along the Fwddog Ridge to Llanthony where St David founded a chapel. Impressed by the beauty and solitude of the valley St David built a simple mud-and-wattle shrine and lived there for many years. When he left his crude hermitage it was forgotten until the closing years of the eleventh century. Riding through the valley in search of game, William de Laci, a retainer of the Earl of Hereford, found the deserted hermitage. Feeling that here was a holy place, he decided to stay there for the rest of his life. His convictions were strong, for one of the early canons of Llanthony wrote that William

> Laid aside his belt and girded himself with a rope; instead of fine linen, he covered himself with haircloth, and instead of his soldier's robe he loaded himself with weighty irons. The suit of armour, which before defended him from the darts of his enemies, he still wore as a garment to harden him against the soft temptations of his old enemy, Satan. That his zeal might not cool, he thus crucified himself, and continued this hard armour on his body until it was worn out with rust and age.

The soldier-monk feared affluence and refused many offers to finance the building of a finer church. When his scruples were overcome, the building of an Augustinian priory was commenced in 1108, dedicated to St John, the patron saint of hermits.

Soon after completion in 1136, the priory became the centre of an incident which was partly responsible for its premature decline. This happened when a Welsh chieftain and his followers sought the right of sanctuary within the priory. His enemies camped

---

The ruins of Llanthony Priory stand on the site of the sixth-century mud-and-wattle shrine erected by St David who for many years lived here in peace and meditation. Erection of the priory began in 1108 and was dedicated to St John, the patron saint of hermits. The architectural style is of the Traditional period—from Norman to Early English

outside, determined to capture him as soon as he came out. The siege prevented supplies being brought in, and as it was difficult to house the refugees the canons were not able to carry out their many religious offices. After making an appeal to the Bishop of Hereford they were given a temporary home at Hereford until a new priory could be built for them at Gloucester. In their new home on the bank of the River Severn they enjoyed royal and noble patronage. This made them reluctant to return to their former home amid the Welsh mountains. They soon forgot the mother-church, and the faithful who remained there suffered hardship and poverty. If the original Llanthony was remembered, it was only as a place of discomfort and penance where offenders were sent to atone for their sins. Referring to the mother-church it was written that

> the monastery was reduced to such straits that the inmates had no surplices—sometimes they had no breeches, and could not, with decency attend Divine service . . . The monks at the daughter-church at Gloucester were revelling in abundance and wealth. They even made sport of our woes and when one was sent hither, would ask, 'what fault has he committed? Why is he sent to prison?' Thus was the mistress and mother-house called a dungeon and a place of banishment to men, as if guilty of every crime.

The mother-church never recovered its former importance, but it managed to remain a place of worship until the Dissolution in the reign of Henry VIII. Although in ruins much of the ancient building remains but little, if anything, can be seen of the daughter-church on the banks of the Severn at Gloucester.

The temperamental poet, Walter Savage Landor (1775–1864), bought the original priory in 1811, intending to lead the agreeable life of a country gentleman. He went so far as to improve the property by planting trees and importing sheep from Spain, but after three years he had quarrelled with so many of his neighbours that he decided to move abroad.

Four miles further up the valley is Capel-y-ffin, where Eric Gill (1882–1940)—the stone-carver, engraver and typographer—lived on a farm during the 1920s, somewhat more peacefully than Landor. Indeed, he chose the spot for its solitude, where he could 'make a cell of good living in the chaos of our world'. A letter to a friend conveys something of the flavour of the place: '2,000 feet of mountain wall on both sides and to the north of it—no outlet but to the south . . . Sheep run on mountains, and stone galore . . . 10 miles to station. Postman on horseback once a day. Doctor on horseback once a week.'

From Llanthony the road runs south through the Vale of Ewyas, meeting the main Abergavenny road at Llanvihangel Crucorney.

The Black Mountains have a pastoral quality, but until the middle of the eighteenth century all the valleys of south-east Wales were just as green and attractive, with hillside farms peopled by folk skilled in weaving and other crafts. The 'black' industries lie hundreds of feet below ground, and the roads between the mining towns twist along the feet of rounded hills, and above them the land is green and pleasant. The mountains were thickly forested until wood was needed to fuel the iron-smelting furnaces, and when coal replaced wood the latter was still required to make props to support the roofs of underground workings. Those who tore the earth apart to extract the ore left awful scars, but they are gradually being covered by grass—a process favoured by the sheep which come down from the mountains in search of anything edible.

Industrialisation brought profit, and the possibilities of making fortunes were endless. South Wales had all that was needed, enabling the owners of furnace and mine to live like princes in fine houses and mock-medieval castles—but the workers were exploited. Conditions of life and work for them became intolerable and in time they combined to resist the insatiable avarice of the industrial barons. The revolutionary growth and events of years ago have left many relics. Apart from being able to see the workings and engines of the recent 'Iron Age' the tourist will appreciate the fine scenery of the hills and valleys which contributed so much to the wealth of Britain. There is no better place to study industrial archaeology than in the valleys of Gwent and Glamorgan, and the local authorities are carrying out a lot of work to uncover the story of the past and present it in the most interesting manner.

Between Abergavenny in Gwent and Neath in West Glamorgan runs the A465 'Heads of the Valleys' road. All the industrial valleys can be entered from this road, for all the valley roads run from north to south. As the valleys are narrow the town layouts are similar, and it is often difficult to know where one town ends and another begins. The shopping areas are in the centre of the valley

39

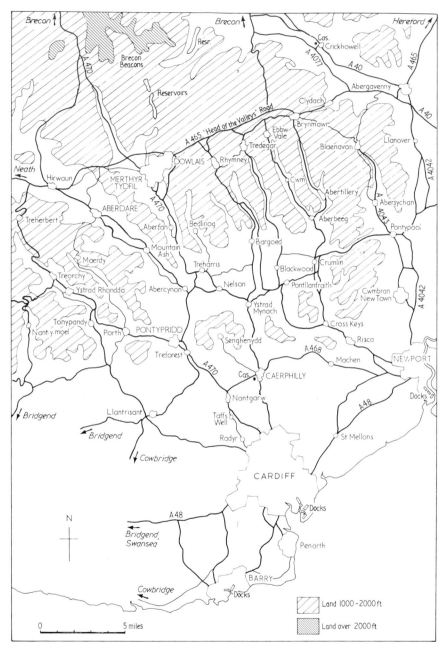

Map 3

floor, the houses rising in close terraces on each side. Behind the houses narrow lanes twist their way along the easiest gradients up to small farms.

The architecture of the valley towns, if similar, is robust, for stone and slate are far more durable materials than the artificial plastic units of present-day mass-production. In recent years a great deal has been done to upgrade the houses. The old up-and-down sash windows have been replaced with modern ones and new entrance doors have a baronial quality. New materials have been selected with care and are in harmony with the main fabric. Woodwork is painted in different colours, the brick surrounds of openings treated to stand out against the grey stonework, and many houses have their fronts cemented and colourwashed in a variety of gay colours. They are more spacious than our modern estate 'boxes', and the miners' fireside tin bathtubs have been replaced by rear-garden extensions which contain the very latest in ablutionary fittings.

If, as they say in these parts, you need a 'toucher', the valley pubs are friendly, and if you have lost your way there is no better place to obtain directions (however confusing) on how to find a road over the mountain from one valley to the next. If it is a Sunday morning the usual inquest is being held on yesterday's rugby game when A. N. Other should have been playing instead of Dai Thomas, who had to be helped home from the pub the night before the match. Dai, they say, kicked the oval ball anywhere but over the horizontal bar between the posts, so he must have been suffering from double-vision.

A good map will show the roads which cross over the mountains from one valley to the next, and from them you will obtain the finest views. Many of the valley towns of Gwent and Rhondda are connected by mountain roads, but before taking them it is wise to make sure they are suitable for cars. Travel down any valley and on the skyline, on one side or the other, you will invariably see the tower of an ancient church. At Mynyddislwyn, between the Sirhowy and Ebbw valleys, the church stands on a hill 1,000ft above sea level. There is a local tradition that St Paul came to this ancient site to preach the Gospel. Perhaps he stood on the tumulus adjoining the present churchyard, a mound claimed by some to be the burial place of a Roman army which was slaughtered by the

An industrial scene in Ebbw Vale

local tribes. Most of the churches stand on prehistoric pagan sites. At the highest point alongside the mountain road between Talywaun and Llanhilleth is one dedicated to St Illtud. The church stands between a pub and a castle motte which, with two other mounds, was known as Castell Taliorum. Being on the line of a Roman road it may have been one of their military stations. It is a cold bleak spot and eerie enough to make one believe that late at night strange noises have been heard and ghostly figures seen standing on the mound. Some folk are certain that the mound is haunted by Roman ghosts, but others, with less imagination, suspect that the local lads, after 'time' has been called at the Carpenter's Arms, are fond of playing pranks.

Within a short distance of the Heads of the Valleys road is Sirhowy where work is being carried out to expose and preserve the furnaces of the ironworks, but it is at Blaenavon that important examples of most of the different kinds of workings connected with the Industrial Revolution can be seen. The old blast furnaces, originally built in 1789, are being restored, and around them are the ruins of the workers' cottages. A mining museum is under construction. Even the town church was built by the local ironmasters, as shown by its iron font and iron-covered tombs. Just over two miles north of Blaenavon is Garnddrys where, as long ago as 1817, a forge worked iron which was then conveyed on trams down a steep mountain incline to the canal wharf at Llanfoist. On a nearby mountainside at Cwmbyrgwm, near Abersychan, is an early (eighteenth century) type of pithead gear in its original position. This raised the coal from the pit by means of a loaded tram balanced against a tank of water. By adjustment of the weight load of the tram and the tank of water the primitive 'lift' went up or down.

The Rhondda area, although possessing the main coal-mining valleys, has few industrial monuments, apart from slag heaps, to remind us of its past importance. A large percentage of Rhondda people now work in other valleys, travelling to the industrial trading estates which have been built at Hirwaun and Treforest. Merthyr Tydfil and Dowlais have more to offer the tourist. At Cefn-Coed and Pontsarn are two great railway viaducts built by the ironmasters across the Taf Fawr and Taf Fechan rivers; the one at Cefn-Coed is one of the largest in Wales. Ruins of blast furnaces still remain, and at Dowlais partially overgrown slag heaps give parts of this area the appearance of a lunar landscape. At Vaynor is a churchyard where one of the 'iron kings' is buried, Robert Thompson Crawshay (1817–79), who gave instructions that his tombstone should be inscribed 'God forgive me'. John Guest owned Dowlais Ironworks and in 1820 built some large stables for his horses. This two-storied building still exists and it is remembered that the upper rooms were used as a school run by Lady Charlotte Guest, translator of the *Mabinogion*.

The houses of the workers were poor. Near the Taff river at Merthy Tydfil are the remains of small terraced dwellings and a chapel built by one of the Crawshay family. It was called Chapel Row, and in one of the poor houses Joseph Parry, the composer, was born in 1841. From his mock-Gothic castle at Cyfarthfa (built in 1824–5) William Crawshay II looked over and ruled his industrial empire, and counted his riches made from the smelting of ore and the casting of cannons which were sent abroad to the wars in France and America. The castle is now a museum containing relics of the 'Iron Age' and many fine works of art. A small model commemorates the occasion in 1804 when Richard Trevithick drove the world's first steam locomotive along the Penydarren Tramway between Merthyr and Abergavenny.

The abandoned workings and rusted skeletal towers supporting huge wheels of winding gear are reminders of past disasters. Just 100 years ago, in a pit at Abercarn, 268 men lost their lives in a violent explosion, and at Senghenydd more than 400 miners were killed in a pit disaster in 1913. But perhaps the greatest tragedy of all took place on a cold grey October morning in 1966 at Aberfan near Merthyr Tydfil. A large tip of waste coal slid down the mountain coming to rest on top of the school and some adjacent houses; 114 children, who had just entered the school, were buried alive. Since this tragedy the heights of coal-tips have been reduced and steps taken to prevent such a disaster happening again.

Whether the tourist is interested in dramatic scenery or industrial archaeology there is a lot to see. Many relics and industrial appliances have been gathered together and placed in the fine Folk Museum at St Fagan's Castle near Cardiff, but it is far more interesting to visit the original sites where the people worked and, if possible, see the tools and machinery they used.

The valleys of North Gwent and Glamorgan offer a double attraction. For students of history there are tangible remains of the recent past, set amid mountains and valleys of great beauty. When Archdeacon Coxe travelled through here in 1808, he wrote:

> We approached the descent to Cwmtillery, and I was surprised with the view of an extensive district well peopled, richly wooded, and highly cultivated, almost rivalling the fertile counties of England. We looked down with delight upon numerous valleys, which abound with romantic scenery, and passed several rills bubbling from the sides of hills and swelling the Tillery. Beneath, at a distance, we saw the littel Ebbw bursting through deep and narrow woody glens and only visible by its foam glistening through the thick foliage.

Although today the mountains and glens are not so thickly wooded there is still much beauty to be seen.

3

Newport and Cardiff,
St Fagan's and Llantrisant

Newport, Casnewydd-ar-Wysg, a few miles from the river mouth, was the most feasible place to ford the Usk and the first crossing was probably made up-river from the present bridge adjacent to the castle. The low marshlands were unattractive so, as in Roman times, the traders went further up the river to Caerleon to discharge their cargoes. When the marshlands were reclaimed a port grew up along the banks of the Usk, and because of its new castle it was named Castell Newydd, but as trade and the size of the town increased it became a 'New Port', and one more convenient than Caerleon. The Normans, seeking a strategic place to cross the river, built a castle to guard it. To do so they must have worked hard to drain and stabilise the marshy ground along both banks of the Usk. Afterwards the Welsh would have been content to name the town Castell Newydd.

The riverside castle was not the first one to be built at Newport, for when the Normans marched into Wales they needed to erect a defensive post as quickly as possible. Without reinforcement, the muddy banks of the Usk were too difficult to build on so a site near Stow Hill was found for a motte-and-bailey fort. Remains of this fort existed until the 1840s when the excavated earth from a new railway tunnel covered it. The later castle was once protected on the town side by a wide moat. It must have been a large fortress for when excavations were made in the High Street, about 200yd away from the main part of the building, portions of the walls of its outer ward were uncovered.

At the start of the nineteenth century the town had little dignity or identity, and its river bridge was 'a weak and miserable fabric trembling at every flow and ebb of the tide'. Now there are three fine bridges: one is near the castle, another is a modern suspension type, while the third is a transporter bridge, opened in 1906 so that

the workers living in the lower part of the town could cross the river to works and factories built along the opposite bank. This fine bridge (there are only three like it in the world) is a landmark for miles around, with 245ft towers, giving 177ft clearance.

In the High Street is the Murenger House, the oldest eating-house and pub in Newport, and about a hundred yards away is Westgate Square where in a rebuilt hotel are two stone pillars which were part of the original building. There are World War II shrapnel marks on the external face of the hotel, but the pillars of the old building are pitted with holes caused by musket fire when the Chartists made an abortive attempt to capture the building from the forces of the Crown in 1839.

From the square Stow Hill climbs to a site where centuries ago a simple mud-and-wattle hermitage stood. As the Norman William de Laci turned from his evil ways to build a church in the Vale of Ewyas so did a Welshman come to this hilltop above Newport to build his simple sanctuary. Gwynllyw, converted by St Tathan of Caerwent from his violent ways, had a vision instructing him to find a hill where there was a white ox with a black spot on its forehead, and there he was to build a church. The little building eventually became a Saxon church until the Normans enlarged and improved it. When they did so the pre-Norman chapel was left to serve as a porch to their new church, now St Woolos Cathedral. The archway they made between the old chapel and the Norman nave is a feature of their skill.

There are few old buildings left within the town; the Murenger House, the Norman castle and the Cathedral of St Woolos are all that remain. The town once had two friaries and a street named Austin Friars in the centre of the town suggests that it was here one of them stood. A large house near the entrance to Belle Vue Park, now part of the Royal Gwent Hospital, is still known as The Friary, and the road leading to it is called Friars Road. Memories

---

The splendid Transporter Bridge at Newport was designed by F. Arnodin, who also built a similar bridge at Marseilles. Two towers, 242ft high, support a platform over the River Usk from which a suspended transporter car crosses the river. It is one of the two such bridges in Britain, the other being at Middlesbrough

of past days surround the town. At Maesglas a modern housing estate stands over the foundations of a castle which could have been seen at the time of the Civil War; houses of another estate stand next to an older Iron Age fortification on Gaer Hill. Not far away is Tredegar House, a large mansion which offered hospitality to King Charles I. At St Julians are the scant remains of another fine house where the illustrious Lord Herbert of Cherbury lived. A church in the same district is named after and dedicated to the honour of two early Christian martyrs Aaron and Julius, who met their deaths in the Roman amphitheatre at Caerleon. A bust of the 'tramp poet', W. H. Davies—'what is life if, full of care . . .'— stands in the art gallery adjoining Newport's museum.

Newport's geographical situation has been its fortune and the town can be regarded as the commercial metropolis of Gwent. Those residents anxious to convince visitors that the area does not lack rural qualities and scenic beauty will take them to see the double-view from Ridgeway. This ridge, on the fringe of a pleasant residential area, divides the town and its industries from the rural outskirts. Here the air is fresh and clean, and it is high enough to look down and over the town. To the south are the green flat moorlands bordering the Bristol Channel, and on the other side of the channel can be seen the shoreline stretching from Somerset as far as the cliffs of north Devon. From the north side of the ridge fields slope down to a green valley where fourteen locks of the old Monmouthshire Canal once enabled barges to enter the industrial waterways of the western valleys of Gwent. Rising above the green fields and the glistening waters of Ynys-y-fro Reservoir is Twm Barlwm at the end of the long ridge of Mynydd Maen. The mountain is near enough to be able to pick out the deep ditch surrounding a large mound which was built as a fort either by the British or the Romans; local folk prefer the theory that it is the burial mound of some important Welsh chieftain.

At Bassaleg on the western outskirts of Newport, where the B4228 joins the A468 road to Caerphilly, is the Ruperra Arms, taking its name from a grey castle standing at the foot of a wooded hill which rises above the Draethen Valley. The sign outside the inn shows the castle, a large square fortress with a circular tower at each of its four corners. Near the inn another road is signposted to Michaelston and Cefn Mabli. Bassaleg is another corner of Gwent offering proof of its historical qualities, for above the roofs of the local grammar school rise the mounds and ditches of an Iron Age fort overlooking the Bristol Channel. On a hill to the south a clump of trees softens the outlines of Maes Arthur fort, and hidden in the folds of other hills are standing stones and burial chambers.

From the village, straight as the flight of an arrow, a road rises several hundred feet to the horizon, following the alignment of one built by the Romans when they came this way from Caerleon through Newport into South Wales. On the horizon is Penylan, a high viewpoint above the lowland moors bordering the Bristol Channel. The panoramic views from here make it easy to appreciate why the Romans engineered their way along this ridgeway between the channel and the southern highlands of Gwent and Glamorgan, a route giving them complete observation over the surrounding countryside.

Near the shoreline are the towers of churches rising above hamlets amid green pastures and not, as in January 1606, surrounded by floodwater when the gale-lashed Severn Sea broke over the sea wall to flood the low-lying land on both sides of the estuary. A great tidal wave swept over the coastal villages drowning many people and their livestock. In a tract of 1607 the Great Flood is described by a writer as,

> The like never in the memory of man hath ever bin seen or heard of . . . townes and villages which suffered great harmes and losses were, Bristol and Aust, and all other countries along both sides of the Severne from Gloster to Bristol, Chepstowe, Matherne, Goldclift, Caldicot Moors, Newport, Cardiff and Swansey. Churches lie hidden in the waters.

Another contemporary account, worth quoting for its Biblical lyricism, states that,

> Huge mighty hills of water tumbling over one another as if the greatest mountains of the world had overwhelmed the low villages and marshy ground. So violent and swift were the outrageous waves that in less than five hours' space of time most parts of these countries, especially the places that lay low, were all overflown, and many hundreds of people, men, women and children were quite devoured; nay more, the farmers and husbandmen and shepherds might behold their goodly flocks swimming upon the waters—dead!

The present sea defences are stronger and considerably higher than those of the seventeenth century, so there is little chance of such a tragedy being repeated.

North of the crossroads at Pant-rhiw-goch is the village of Michaelston-y-Fedw, and a short distance away a tree-lined drive curves up a gentle slope to the mansion of Cefn Mabli, its southern façade representing two architectural periods, Tudor and Georgian. Its main reception hall is T-shaped and once had a raised dais above the main floor. In feudal times the lord of the manor sat here with his family and privileged guests, the retainers and lesser folk sitting at tables on the lower floor, 'below the salt'. Originally the floor was stone, replaced at a later date with wide planks of seasoned oak, and the present wall panels cover ones of the Tudor period. Being difficult to heat in cold weather it once had three

The Mansion of Cefn Mabli. Cefn Mabli means 'Mable's Ridge', perpetuating the name of the daughter of Robert Fitzhamon, Earl of Gloucester, who built the first house here. During the Civil War the present mansion resisted attack from Ironside troops who were beaten off by Sir Nicholas Kemeys who was later killed when defending Chepstow Castle

fireplaces; now there is only one, bearing the arms and motto of the Kemeys family—Duw dy eas, meaning 'God Thy Grace'.

Many of these old houses have secret passages and chambers. Behind a well-concealed hinged panel, steps lead down to a small vault from which a passage is said to have gone underground to the River Rhymney. This escape route would have allowed many a fugitive to elude his pursuers, so the story that King Charles I made use of it should not be dismissed. Eventually the passage became an egress for rats and it was closed. Above the secret chamber is a box-like hiding place just large enough for one person to stand in. These small hiding places were used in the days when priests sought shelter from religious persecution.

High above the well of the main staircase is a large beam; apart from its structural function it was used as a hanging-beam for the execution of criminals after trial and conviction at the local courthouse (now the vicarage) at Michaelston-y-Fedw. The stairwell formed a vertical shaft through which the bodies dropped to a stone-flagged floor below. The lord of the manor did not always wait for the offender to be brought to trial; as he held absolute power over his serfs justice was often quick and rough.

Above the 'hanging staircase' is a long narrow room known as the 'dancing gallery'. It must have been used for dancing for an old Welsh verse praises the terpsichorean ability of Sir Charles Kemeys who was considered to be one of the best dancers in Wales. The verse says:

> The best three dancers in Wales,
> Sir Charles of Cefn Mabli,
> Squire Lewis of the Fan,
> And Sir John Carne of Ewenny.

A small room next to the 'dancing gallery' is called the 'priest's room', so it might have been used as a confessional. Perhaps those sentenced to be suspended from the black beam over the staircase were allowed time to seek forgiveness for their sins and a blessing from the priest before being led away to stand under the improvised gallows. This is possible, for it is said that on the Eve of St John the sound of feet have been heard making their way along the planked floors towards the confessional.

Queen Elizabeth I and King Charles I were great tourists for

51

they seem to have occupied bedrooms in most historic houses in Britain—Charles, of course, from necessity (particularly after the Battle of Naseby), so it is not surprising that there is a chamber here known as the 'King's Room'.

Robert Fitzhamon, Earl of Gloucester, built the first house, naming it after his daughter Mabel, for the translation of Cefn Mabli is 'Mabel's Ridge'. The house is also associated with the Norman Stephen de Kemeys who lived in Gwent between 1234 and 1241. Stephen must have liked the Welsh for he allowed his wife to name their first son Iorweth. During the Civil War the mansion was attacked by Ironside troops, but they were beaten off by Sir Nicholas Kemeys, a brave man who met a hero's death when defending Chepstow Castle against the Ironsides.

From Michaelston-y-Fedw, where the church is reputed to stand on the site of a Roman post, the road soon crosses the Rhymney river. Just after crossing over the river bridge a lane on the left leads to Ruperra Castle. Built on the lower slopes of Coed Craig Ruperra, 300ft to 400ft above sea level, the castle with its four towers backed by the Craig is an impressive structure. Square in plan, three storeys high and with a round tower at each corner it resembles a Norman keep. There is little ornamentation, except to the south porch which bears the arms of the Morgan family and the date of 1602. It is claimed that the castle was designed by the famous architect Inigo Jones, who had Welsh connections; as he and Sir Thomas Morgan were Royalists it is feasible that he did design and supervise the constructional work. Old photographs show it to have been a comfortable home. It is one of those places where a plaque might have been hung stating that 'King Charles I slept here', for he is supposed to have stayed at the castle for two nights after the Battle of Naseby, his bedroom being known as the 'King's Chamber'. It is quite surprising how many historic houses claim to have sheltered that unhappy monarch after the fatal battle.

Twice the castle has been gutted by fire, the first occasion being in 1783. It had several fine interior features, among them a Georgian staircase and a Great Hall with a minstrel gallery on which the date of the first fire was recorded together with the date of restoration—1789. In the early stages of the last war the interior was destroyed for the second time. On 8 December 1941 the *Western Mail* reported that:

In recent months Ruperra Castle was occupied by the military. A fire broke out on an upper floor. Soldiers made a dramatic escape, but one soldier, being trapped, jumped from a third floor window to the ground fifty feet below. He was seriously injured. The fire could be seen from Cardiff and Newport. Fortunately all the treasures the building contained had been removed years ago.

The road from the ill-fated castle, which has not been restored, follows the Rhymney river northwards to Draethen village, then crosses the river again to join the main Caerphilly to Newport road at Lower Machen. Not far from this road junction is Plas Machen, a house whose Tudor gables and windows are a reminder that a past owner had joined forces with Henry Tudor on his march to defeat King Richard III on Bosworth Field in 1485.

This journey along a Roman road above the moors and through a sequestered hinterland makes an interesting day—a day 'to stand and stare' and one of variety, memory and enchantment.

The recorded history of Cardiff begins in 1079 but it must have been a place of habitation long before then, for the stone axes of prehistoric man have been found on a hill at Penylan, and in the sixth century there was a Celtic colony at Ely. Soon after the Romans founded Isca Silurum (Caerleon) they built a fort on the east bank of the Taff, so Caer-Taff might have been the early name for Cardiff. The walls of a Norman castle rise from Roman stonework, but it was not until the twelfth century that Cardiff became a known town, important enough to be encircled by a system of outer defences—some of them built on the earthworks of prehistoric man and on the remains of Roman fortifications. At St Mellons was Caer Castell; near Llanishen another camp was improved by the Normans. Others were built at Whitchurch, Dinas Powis and Rhiwbina. A mound at the latter is supposed to cover the remains of Iestyn ap Gwrgan, a Welsh prince slain here in a battle so fierce that a neighbouring stream is called Nant Waedlyd, 'the bloody brook'.

There are many stories and legends of Celtic saints setting up shrines in riverside hollows and lonely valleys, and of how the Norman knights made a rapacious division of Glamorgan and Gower. There were other unwelcome visitors, one being Owain Glyndwr, and a visit from him usually meant trouble. Then

Cromwell came to bombard the town and the castle, and not long afterwards horses pulled a black hearse-like coach through Cardiff taking the evil-tempered Judge Jeffreys to court the widow of Philip Jones of Fonmon Castle.

Towards the end of the thirteenth century, the castle was extended and strengthened by Gilbert de Clare. In the late eighteenth century the Bute family undertook the restoration and preservation work, enormous amounts of money being expended to create the interior grandeur that can be seen today. The Bute family also spent large sums on the development of the town itself, in particular on dock construction.

Cardiff people have reason to be proud of the fine buildings of its Civic Centre. Just over one hundred years ago, the first civic building, which was built in the fourteenth century, still stood in the middle of the High Street. It was described as being:

> A faire Towne Hall, wherein is holden the Town Court every fortnight. Adjoining the same is a faire Shambles below, wherein Victuals are sold: and above a faire great Chamber, where Ye Aldermen and Magistrates use to consult: and under the Hall is the Prison, wherein offenders and misdoers are committed.

The word 'shambles' should not be misunderstood for it means meat market. The entrance to the present market is almost opposite where the old Town Hall once stood, a small building measuring but 46ft by 26ft, yet large enough to accommodate the Justices and administrators of Cardiff—and there was room for a prison. Executions took place in front of the Town Hall; a poor fisherman named White was burnt at the stake, and another unfortunate man, a Jesuit priest, suffered the same fate.

Features of this century's new towns are the covered ways to shops, but Cardiff has provided such shelter to shoppers over many years for there are more arcades here, off St Mary's Street, than in many other towns.

If cheap fruit and vegetables are required Mill Lane is the place to go, where goods are displayed on open stalls. This street follows the line of the old city wall, and alongside it a canal once ran. This waterway conveyed raw materials and the engines of war to be shipped from Cardiff docks for use in America and France, a trade which brought prosperity and necessitated larger docks.

The National Museum of Wales, completed in 1927, houses a rich selection of objects illustrating Welsh history and culture, together with French Impressionist paintings. The town has some 440 acres of parks and open spaces. For sportsmen there is Cardiff Arms Park, a modern amphitheatre where, encouraged by the battle-songs of leek- and daffodil-decorated supporters, the men of Wales continue their battles with foes from the other side of Offa's Dyke. National feelings run high, but today the encounters are sporting and very little blood is spilt.

Llandaff is Cardiff's most important suburb, with a history that cannot be separated from that of the mother-city. Only a short way from the hustle and bustle of the busy streets of Cardiff, it has managed to retain the dignity of a small and quiet village. Around the Cathedral Green with its medieval Preaching Cross are elegant well-maintained houses, and the ruined towers of a Norman gatehouse remind one that in the past the village streets had echoed to the sound of marching men and the clash of steel.

Important in history, if not in size, a Llandaff church has always dominated this spot near the banks of the River Taff, for here the first small church was built on a site reputed to be one of the earliest monastic foundations in Britain. Close to the river and in the shelter of a hill, St Teilo set up a cross in a mud-and-wattle sanctuary, and he probably enclosed it to protect himself from wild beasts and even wilder humans. This enclosure he would have called a *llan* which eventually became one of the Welsh words for 'church'

In the eleventh century a stone-built structure was begun to replace the primitive hermitage of St Teilo. Since then it has been rebuilt and enlarged several times, but basically the church seen today is the one which existed near the end of the thirteenth century. During the Civil War it suffered the indignity of serving as a pub for the troops of Cromwell, and years afterwards two great storms caused considerable damage. Along the external face on the south side at eaves height are projecting stone corbels, each one faced with the sculptured head of every king and queen of England since the Norman Conquest. All wear royal crowns, except the last head which is that of King Edward VIII who of course did not attend a coronation ceremony. There is a story that after the last corbel has been sculptured and there is no space left for another one, the building will fall. In 1941 the Germans dropped a large land-mine which caused great damage to the south side of the building, but fortunately the line of royal heads remained intact and they still look over the churchyard.

In the centre of the cathedral, dominating the interior, is a huge parabolic-shaped concrete arch supporting a sculptured aluminium figure of Christ. The arms of the huge figure stretch out over the nave as if in welcome, and the upturned palms seem to offer a benediction. The presentation is deeply symbolic; the sculptured features of the Saviour's face are unmistakably Hebrew, with large eyes and an expression of ineffable sadness. It is awesome but strangely not frightening. Some may find the impact disturbing, but it is certainly a masterpiece of contemporary ecclesiastical art. Not slavishly copying the dictates of past fashion, Sir Joseph Epstein has truly captured the majesty of Christ. The figure conveys a sense of acceptance and understanding. Its conception is modern but in complete harmony with the early architectural qualities of the ancient building. Many have condemned it out of hand; it needs to be seen several times before forming a final opinion of its merit.

A minor unclassified road runs through Fairwater, west of Cardiff, along a ridge overlooking the Ely river to St Fagan's, a place where one of the biggest battles ever fought in Wales took place. This decisive Civil War battle occurred in some fields north-west of the village in 1648. Long before this bloody battle took place the village had been disturbed by marauding Danes and Saxons, and after them by the Normans as they fought to establish themselves in South Wales. Relics of these encounters have been discovered in nearby woods and pastures. The castle of St Fagan's is now a splendid National Folk Museum—a fine building and much more comfortable than the original one on this mound above the Ely river; the latter was built about 1560 but in the north façade are parts of an earlier fortress built by Sir Peter le Sore.

It is not recorded that Queen Elizabeth I visited the castle, but King Charles I certainly did when he came to recruit an army. His efforts were successful only after he promised to redress the complaints of the local people and to drive the Papists out of the country. Two years after his visit eight thousand men marched to meet the troops of Cromwell in battle, but the pressed men, ill-armed and led by local squires, were no match for the well-trained Ironsides. Although the battle lasted only two hours, the King's army was almost wiped out of existence. Those who managed to escape from the battlefield where 'a brook ran red with blood' must have remembered the terror of this May morning for the rest of their lives.

A new museum accommodates items which could not be easily displayed inside the castle; in the expansive grounds are many interesting buildings brought from different parts of Wales. There is an old woollen mill from Llanwrtyd Wells, complete with its original machinery; a thatched cottage from Flintshire, and one built of large boulder-pebbles from Dolgellau. Sporting days, too, have been remembered (although not a sport to everyone's taste) in the erection of a circular cockpit, complete in every detail.

Inside the museum are more recent relics, weapons and implements of peace and war. There are frightening displays of old surgical instruments. Folk culture is represented, art and craft, love and birth. There are Welsh love spoons carved by young men in proof of undying affection, some dating back to the seventeenth century. One item supporting a Welsh superstition is a piece of translucent tissue which covers the head of some babies at birth. This strange head-covering is called a caul, and it is claimed that whoever carries one will never die from drowning, and will also have the dubious gift of being able to see and converse with spirits.

The main road from St Fagan's runs from the entrance gates of the castle northwards to Llantrisant, passing through Radyr and Pentyrch. From the latter place it is about two miles to the hilltop site of 'the Church of the Three Saints'. *Llan* is the Welsh word for church, *tri* means three, and *sant* means saint—so the logical name for the village could only have been Llantrisant.

From the east the Romans brought war and a new culture with them into Wales, but from the west in later years the Celtic saints came in peace and brought a new religion. This spot must have been favoured for *three* saints to climb the steep hillside to establish a *llan* and persuade the heathens to put aside their pagan gods and accept conversion to Christianity. The holy men could not have found a more exposed place on which to build an enclosure. It had to be strong enough to withstand the most fierce gale, and stout enough to keep out the warlike people from a settlement on an adjoining hill. These were savage times, so it is unlikely that these early Celtic saints were always willing to 'offer the other cheek'. As a prophet of old called to heaven for fire to destroy the false god of Baal, it seems that the concerted efforts of the three saints were able to persuade the primitive tribes to accept a new way of life, and it is certain that they knew a trick or two to frighten them. In time a church was built inside the *llan* and dedicated to the three saints; Illtud, Wonno and Tyfodwg.

The Normans favoured this hilltop site, and after completing their castle probably sent the same masons to build a new and better church on the site of the old one. When a Norman castle was attacked it was usual for the church to suffer too, especially if its tower had defensive features. As Llantrisant Church had to be rebuilt in the sixteenth century it can be assumed that not all damage to it was caused by storm and time. The foundations of the castle were laid in 1147. During the ensuing years it was attacked many times, but in 1326 one of its towers was still considered safe enough to imprison an English king. When his queen had news that Edward II and his favourite, the young Despenser, were in hiding at Neath Abbey she sent the Earl of Lancaster with an army to arrest him. To escape them Edward set out for Caerphilly Castle, but on the way he was captured and imprisoned at Llantrisant before being sent to Berkeley Castle near Gloucester where he met his death in a dungeon about ten months later.

The historian Malkin did not have a very good opinion of Llantrisant. He wrote,

> This town has everything about it except situation, lying out of the high road between Cardiff and Merthyr Tydfil and at the begining of hilly country, its intercourse with the Vale is very limited and irregular!

Anyway the town must have been a healthier place than in the eighteenth century for then it was said:

> That vapours from ye mines are causes of fatal diseases, and that unless the many pits were filled in most of the town and parts of it will die!

It is recorded that in a period of thirteen months two hundred people did die.

At the beginning of the nineteenth century the atmosphere must have improved for Dr William Price, druid and sun-worshipper, found the town very much to his taste. He will always be remembered as the pioneer of cremation. The doctor was also a supporter of the Chartist movement, his activities in this cause making it necessary for him to flee to France to avoid arrest and deportation. After some years he returned, but so unconventional was his mode of life and morals that he built himself a tower at Pontypridd, a type of residence that he considered safer than a normal house. Incensed by his strange behaviour the angry townspeople attacked the tower, causing Dr Price to escape by hiding in a laundry basket.

After this incident he returned to Llantrisant where he lived in a cottage with a young girl who bore his child. He was eighty-three when his child was born and he named it Iesu Grist (Jesus Christ) and when the boy died at an early age the old doctor, who considered himself above the law, set up a pyre on a hill above the town to burn the body. The police rushed up the hill and arrested him for his unlawful attempt to dispose of a body. At his trial, in 1884, so successful was his defence that cremation became established as a legal act. Ten years later he died at the age of ninety-three, and his deathbed request that his body be cremated was carried out—on the same hill where he had built a funeral pyre for his infant son. The name of Dr Price is inseparable from that of Llantrisant.

4

The Vales of Neath and Glamorgan

Memorial sites are marked on several maps, but many of the most interesting relics have been removed and set up in museums. A museum at Margam contains a collection of the prehistoric stones and Celtic crosses which once stood alongside the ancient trackways across the hills of South Wales. Crosses commemorated important events, and others were used as gravestones or to mark the extent of a gift of land. Standing stones came from unlikely places; one circular stone served as a pier at the entrance to a farm, and another two stones placed side by side were used as a footbridge. The Margam Museum houses tall stones inscribed with names of local chieftains, and there are Celtic crosses dating from the sixth century.

At Margam are the ruins of a Cistercian abbey, a building said to have been more splendid than Tintern in the Wye Valley. From here overgrown trackways lead to burial mounds and earthworks on the surrounding hills. Not far away from the centre of the town, on Mynydd Castell, is a large oval-shaped encampment. Many of the towns lying along the coastal belt with their oil refineries, tinplate and steel works are unpleasant places to linger in, for they often lie under a thick pall of industrial smoke and the atmosphere is tainted with a granular dust. In the cause of a healthy economy this must be accepted, for as they say up north, 'where there's muck there's brass'.

The Cistercians, who were skilled agriculturists, made certain to build their monastic houses in places where the fields were rich, and near a river which could supply them with plenty of pure water and good fish. Neath was such a place, and the land behind their abbey with its thickly wooded gorges and high waterfalls would have pleased them too, for here nature has carved out a landscape even more beautiful than the Cistercian building which Leland described as 'the most beautiful abbey in all Wales'.

When the Romans began to engineer their military roads

through South Wales their main highway went across the River Rhymney to Roath, and then to Caerau where they built a station; always, as far as possible, keeping in sight of the Bristol Channel, the road went on to Neath, a place which they called Nidum.

Between Cardiff and Neath several minor roads left the main military highway to climb northwards up to the mountain ridges. The best known of these roads, and perhaps the most used, was the Sarn Helen, or 'Helen's Causeway'. This was built at the request of a queen who, according to tradition and the *Mabinogion*, married an Emperor of Rome. Helen is supposed to have had three castles built for her, and when she requested a fine straight road to run between them the Sarn was laid down. Up to about two hundred years ago it was the main route between Neath and Brecon.

For exploration of the hill country to the north, Neath is a central point. One road, the A474, goes through the mountains to Pontardwe and the Swansea Valley. From Pontardwe it is possible to go over the mountains to Sennybridge and Brecon. This road, the A4067, runs through the uplands of Fforest Fawr; along the way is Craig-y-nos Castle, once the home of the legendary Adelina Patti, the world-famous opera singer. The castle was equipped with a magnificent theatre where occasionally Madam Patti, with other famous singers, sang opera. Here must have been the Welsh Glyndebourne, although the audiences were invited guests. Near the castle are caves which rival those at Cheddar in Somerset; their guidebook claiming that this is one outing that even a rainy day fails to mar. You have no need to crawl, climb or clamber for easy paths have been made and all is brightly illuminated by electricity.

If a spot where natural beauty has not been commercialised is preferred, take a lane off the A4067 from Pen-y-cae up to Coelbren where Sgwd-Henrhyd waterfall thunders over a cliff 100ft above the Tawe river. This is the highest waterfall in this part of South Wales. At Coelbren is another Roman marching camp, and from it the Sarn Helen can still be followed across the moors to Brecon.

The most used road is the A465 running north-east through the Vale of Neath to Hirwaun. About six miles along this road is Resolven where a narrow lane alongside the Melin Court brook leads to a ravine where another waterfall makes a spectacular 80ft drop. The Clydach brook runs through a gorge between the

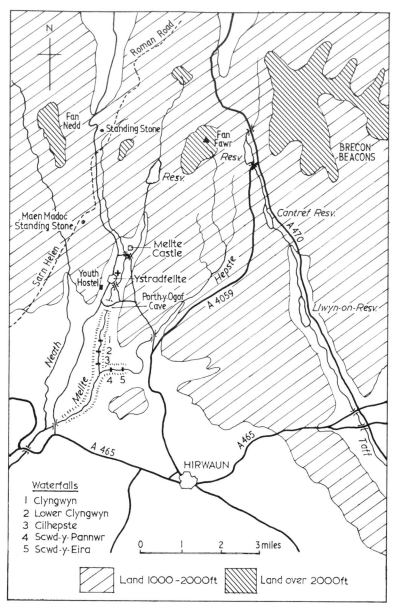

N

Roman Road

Fan
Nedd

• Standing Stone

Fan
Fawr

Resv.

BRECON
BEACONS

Resv.

Cantref Resv.

Maen Madoc
Standing Stone

A 470

Sarn Helen

Mellte
Castle

Hepste

Llwyn-on-Resv.

Youth
Hostel

Ystradfellte

A 4059

Neath

Port-y-Ogof
Cave

1
2
3
4 5

Mellte

A 465

A 465

Taff

HIRWAUN

Waterfalls
1 Clyngwyn
2 Lower Clyngwyn
3 Cilhepste
4 Scwd-y-Pannwr
5 Scwd-y-Eira

0   1   2   3 miles

Land 1000-2000ft   Land over 2000ft

Map 4

mountains, and the wooded heights of Hir Fynydd are cleft with clear running streams and other waterfalls. Along the ridge of Hir Fynydd the old Roman road runs down to the square-shaped Gaer at Coelbren. The scenic beauty and historic interest of these upland heights is inexhaustible. Our ancestors built their settlements here and ancient stones and mounds mark the sites of their battles.

Other impressive cataracts can be found at the north-eastern end of the vale where the Nedd and Mellte rivers join at Pont Nedd Fechan. The river gorges are deep and one of them ends at the waterfall of Ysgwyd Einon Gam. Just past Glyn Neath a minor road leaves the A465 to run along a ridge following the Neath river northwards to its source on Fan Gihiych. On the western side of the ridge the Mellte river, after being joined by the Llia, flows from its birthplace on the lower slope of Fan Llia. After passing a Youth Hostel the road reaches the small village of Ystradfellte. Near the Youth Hostel a narrow lane runs down to a conveniently placed car park at the top of a gorge. At the bottom of the gorge is a large cave called Porth-yr-Ogof which forms a 300yd tunnel over the Mellte river. At one time this great cavern, said to be the largest in Wales, was called the White Horse Cave because calcite streaks on the rock wall, about 100ft or so inside the cave, resemble the head of a white horse.

Any romantically minded visitor will savour the legend surrounding the ghostly equine head, which tells how a Welsh princess, fearing the worst possible fate if her hot-breathed panting pursuer should catch her, rode her white horse through the ravine in an effort to escape. Near the cave entrance the horse stumbled, both rider and steed being thrown into a river pool and drowned. The calcite deposits on the rock, which are certainly the same shape as a horse's head, must have encouraged someone to tell this story which could have come straight out of the *Mabinogion*.

The waterfalls of these river gorges are so beautiful that they deserve more than a passing mention, and it is not necessary to travel through the valley from Neath to find them. The area can easily be reached from Brecon or Merthyr. It lies just over the boundary from the industrial valleys of north Glamorgan and among the mountains of Fforest Fawr in Powys. Bleak and very exposed, this is a lonely, boggy tract of land. All the Fforest Fawr peaks are over 2,000ft high, and from the rain-soaked ground between them spring the rivers of Hepste and Mellte which meet near the waterfall of Scwd yr Eira to flow south-west to join the River Neath. The upland moors between the valleys of Tawe and Cwm Taff are cleft by the deep wooded gorges of Hepste and Mellte. To find and appreciate the various fascinating features of this area, which can only be explored on foot, the OS Sheet, Brecon Beacons, No 160 is essential.

Almost halfway between Brecon and Merthyr, the A4059 climbs to the moorlands of Fforest Fawr. The weather here is often stormy and changeable and the Brecon Beacon heights of Corn Du and Pen-y-fan are frequently veiled in black clouds with long ragged streamers lying like dark shrouds over the saddle between the peaks. If this part of the journey is by car the ride over the open moorland above the river gorges is exhilarating. There is a wild beauty about this strange land of Fforest Fawr where there are tracks so old that even the Romans thought them ancient and, approving their alignment, overlaid them when they constructed their Sarn Helen across the moors of Powys and Dyfed.

At a roadside clearing a lane is signposted to Ystradfellte. From here a walk across the tufty ground reaches a point where it is possible to cross the upper stream of the Hepste river. The route passes alongside water courses flanked with stunted trees and bushes, past worn and rusted agricultural implements to the ruins of a deserted farmhouse. From here the ground slopes to the edge of the Mellte ravine, 100ft above the Clungwyn Fall. The placid Mellte becomes turbulent as the green-tinted water foams and swirls before cascading over a rocky ledge. A narrow goat track snakes diagonally down the side of the ravine to the top of the fall, then continues to its foot some 60ft below.

The spectacular Clungwyn, as if reluctant to lose its former grandeur, becomes reincarnated in miniature before the rushing water dwindles to a more tranquil course. A deep pool bars the way making it necessary to clamber over a scree of tumbled rocks and fallen trees to reach a higher level at the edge of an escarpment above the ravine. Below is the watersmeet of the river valleys of Mellte and Hepste, and the lower Cilhepste Fall. 'Cil', derived from 'Cul', means narrow—and as the river tumbles through a V-

The Waterfall of Scwd y Eira. From a rocky ledge, 60–70ft high, Scwd y Eira, 'The Spout of Snow', cascades down into the river below. It is possible to walk along a narrow ledge and stand behind this torrent of white water

shaped cleft the fall is aptly named. The rough path winds through the trees to reach the river bank at the head of the lower Cilhepste Fall, the narrow valley bottleneck opening out so that the gorge is wide enough to contain the river and paths on both sides.

On emerging from the trees you will see in front of you the grandest and most magnificent of the Mellte and Hepste falls. Rising some 60 to 70ft above the river a torrent of white water cascades down into a river pool, foaming and swirling as the terrific force of the water causes it to rise in clouds of misty spray. This is Scwd-yr-Eira, 'the Spout of Snow'. The falls seem to bar the way out of the gorge, but there is a track which goes up the side of the ravine to the moors. After the close confinement of the deep gorges and the insistent noise of the rivers and falls this is a magic path up to a new land—a land where the cries of sheep and curlew seem strange and unfamiliar.

The Mellte is located again near the village of Ystradfellte. To find this village today is not too difficult, but centuries ago many of the Marcher Lords, summoned by their king to come here for a conference, failed to find it. A short way to the north the map is marked with the names of two castles—Castell Coch and Mellte Castle. This is confusing, but it is generally accepted that both names refer to one castle, the Mellte. There is little trace of it now, but *if* this is one of the stone castles built at the demand of Helen it is possible that during the years after the Roman occupation its walls were dismantled and the stones used in other buildings. Many stone castles have disappeared, but older earthworks have remained.

On the horizon, between the mountains of Fan Nedd and Fan Llia, is a tall standing stone—Maen Llia—possibly put up by ancient man to indicate that here was a pass between the mountains and the way into the Senni Valley. On the left of the mountain road a rough track goes across the open moorland. This was no ordinary track, but was the Roman Sarn Helen coming across the moors from Coelbren. Here and there are traces of the original Roman pavé, and there is another standing stone—Maen Madoc. It bears a Latin inscription—DERVAC FILLIVS, on one edge, and on the other IVST JACIT. The lettering is worn but an acceptable translation is DEURACIUS SON OF JUSTIN, HE LIES HERE. It was probably a typical roadside burial in the Roman manner, the prehistoric stone being used as a memorial.

From Maen Llia, the Roman road continues over the moors, around Fan Frynych and across Mynydd Illtud into southern Breconshire. Just beyond the prehistoric stone the mountain road, with several hairpin bends, goes steeply down the mountainside into the Senni Valley. From the top of the descent there is a spectacular view of this lush valley backed by the foothills of Mynydd Eppynt. The wild upland between the Vale of Neath and the Vale of Senni is a strange and eerie place. All around are miles of open windswept moorland with the lines of ancient trackways running between prehistoric settlements.

The Vale of Glamorgan is an area of pastoral beauty which lies between the A48 trunk road and the Bristol Channel. Inside the Vale a criss-cross complexity of lanes runs in all directions, linking

Tinkinswood Burial Chamber is one of the largest and best preserved megalithic chambered tombs in Britain. The enormous capstone is 3ft thick and weighs about 40 tons. It was once covered by a large elongated earthen tumulus

picturesque villages and sleepy little hamlets. From a roundabout at the junction of the roads from St Fagan's and Barry, the A48 climbs up to the Downs. Troops using the Downs during the last war were not aware that they had put up their tents on the same site used by the Royalist troops before they marched down the Tumble to the Battle of St Fagan's on 8 May 1648. The fields around this spot must have been the scene of many a bloody skirmish. Exhausted after a hard battle, and many without arms, a large number of these Royalists were slaughtered by the Ironsides who pursued them up the Tumble from St Fagan's. It was a massacre, and for years afterwards when the land was dug for drainage a number of bones and skulls were found, most of them bearing scars made by the vicious slashing strokes of pike and sword.

The A48 trunk road serves as a convenient spine from which

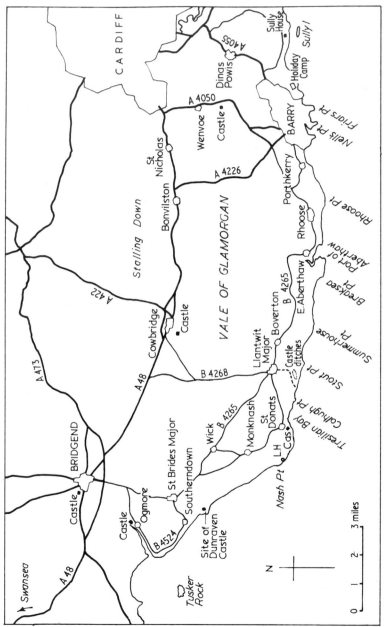

Map 5

lanes run southward into the Vale of Glamorgan, their direction through pretty tree-lined valleys being governed by the meandering ways of streams and rivers. Such a lane runs from St Nicholas to Tinkinswood where are the remains of one of the largest Neolithic burial chambers in Britain. This huge chamber could have been fashioned by men who landed on the nearby coast and settled here about 2500 BC. One feels uneasy in this place, especially if this site of sepulchre is visited at the time of an unexpected storm, and black clouds begin to darken the sky.

A similar atmosphere did not deter a local drunk who, according to legend, overcome by alcohol fell asleep under the projecting capstone. The ghosts haunting this spot objected to their last resting-place being treated as a common doss-house, so they seized upon the drunken fellow by his hair and whirled him high above the earth until he was dropped in the middle of Dyffryn Woods. He must have survived this rough treatment otherwise the story of his horrific experience would not have been known.

Nearby is St Lythan's where there is another prehistoric tomb. There is no story here of any human being whirled through the sky, but a strange legend insists that the large capstone rises above its supports once every year and 'whirleth around thrice'. No reason has ever been given for this strange performance.

After the village of St Nicholas the next lane into the Vale leaves the A48 at Bonvilston. It passes a spot known locally as Liege Castle which could have referred to an old Roman camp, possibly called Legion's Castle. The lane follows the Nant Whitton stream to Llancarfan, one of the most fascinating villages in the Vale. In the years following the Roman occupation Llancarfan became a centre of Celtic monasticism and one of the holiest sites in Wales.

The origins of several early Celtic churches are connected with stories of animals. At Newport, St Gwynllyw built his sanctuary on a hill where he was told to seek a white ox. In the sixth century St Cadoc came to this quiet valley where he laid the foundations of Llancarfan Abbey on a site where he disturbed a wild boar. There is little doubt that the present church stands on and over the foundations of St Cadoc's abbey. As early prehistoric settlements overlook the village, this area must have been occupied many years before St Cadoc disturbed the boar.

A steep hill curves upwards from Llancarfan to Pancross,

turning southwards with the Nant Whitton stream to Penmark where a Norman church has lasted longer than the invaders' castle. When the Roundheads bombarded the castle from the heights of Castle Ditches they must have had great artillery expertise to avoid hitting and destroying the church. Evidence that they placed their guns here during the Civil War is substantiated by the fact that several skeletons, fragments of rusted weapons, armour and a horse's bit and stirrup were found here about 1850.

When one of the Norman lords who helped Earl Robert Fitzhamon conquer Glamorgan wanted a site for his castle he found one at Fonmon, and on it he built a strong fortress which, in the event of an attack, could be supported by others at Penmark, Castleton and East Orchard. In Norman times it was known as Foulmont Castle. With its massive walls nearly 5ft thick, part of the original castle remains. Despite expansion and reconstruction over a period of several centuries it has been continually occupied ever since it was built. Descendants of the first owner, William St John, lived here until about the middle of the seventeenth century, then in 1656 the castle with its estates were sold to Colonel Philip Jones.

The Georgian period library has one of the finest rococo ceilings in Wales, while in the large kitchen a dresser displays a collection of fine pewter, and on one wall are the remains of a dog-spit, or wheel. Fine works of art are hung in many rooms; in the entrance hall is a portrait of Oliver Cromwell painted by Robert Walker.

Half a mile west of Bonvilston is a place marked on the map as Greenway, an appropriate name for all lanes into the Vale. One lane leads to the small hamlet of Llantryddyd where there is a ruined mansion and yet another church dedicated to St Illtud, a favoured saint in this part of Wales. Some of the more important deceased residents of the parish have memorials inside the church. These show the visitor what they looked like and the sort of clothing they wore, while inscriptions give details of their lives and titles. The Llantryddyd memorial-tomb is dated 1597, showing Sir John Basset and Elizabeth his wife looking down on the recumbent figures of their daughter and son-in-law. Anthony Mansel lies by the side of his wife, and around the ornate tomb are the 'weepers'—the seven Mansel children in period dress. A sad and simpler memorial was set up in the churchyard by a native of

Neath who brought his child here for burial. The gravestone states that his *thirty-sixth* child rests here.

Adjoining the churchyard is a rutted nettle-covered field, all that remains of the once-well-kept gardens of a fine manor house which is now a grey gaunt ruin. Plas Llantryddyd was a fine example of a Tudor squire's home, but in less than three hundred years after it was built the roof fell in, and the villagers carried away the fallen stones and timbers for use in other buildings. Long dark shadows cast by the tower of the ancient church and the ruins of the Plas give one the feeling that this is a cold and haunted spot, but perhaps not as haunted as a nearby hollow called Pantylladron—'The Hollow of Thieves'. These thieves were highwaymen who waylaid travellers making their way on foot along the high ridge above the Vale. Coaches on their way from Cardiff to Cowbridge were also held up by the masked highwaymen, then it was a case of 'your money or your life', and more often it was both. Ghosts of the murdered travellers are said to haunt this hollow above the hamlet of Llantryddyd.

Above Cowbridge is Stalling Down, another place which may well be haunted and with greater reason. It was here, in 1400, that Glyndwr and his men fought one of their greatest battles against the English. The encounter must have been particularly fierce for an old account of it states that 'blood was up to the horse's fetlocks'. The exact site and date of the battle is shown on the early inch scale OS map of the district.

Not far away is the village of St Hilary on a knoll above the river Thaw. To the south is a bridge at Howe Mill from where a path goes across the fields to one of the most interesting castles in the Vale. At Beaupre the Sitsyllts founded a dynasty from which a Marshal of England descended, and they were the forefathers of the famous Cecils. It is claimed that the Lords of Beaupre Castle, with several important Welshmen, joined the barons in drafting the Magna Carta. A story difficult to prove, but as King John was supposed to have hidden from his barons in a secret room at Boverton Castle there may be some truth in it.

The Welsh called Boverton Tre Befered, but finding this difficult the Normans changed it to Bogarton, from which presumably derived the present-day Boverton. A ruin in the village is known as a castle but perhaps, or so the story goes, this is because (as mentioned above) King John hid there from his barons who were pestering him to sign the Magna Carta. If the barons did meet at Beaupre to prepare the charter then the story may be true. When news got round the village that the stranger who called himself Gerald Fitzgerald was, in fact, their king, the Plas was described as a castle—Trebenin, 'The Place of Kings'. John's divorced wife Hawise lived there, but it is not known what pressure he put upon her to hide him. If the story is true that soon after her death she began to haunt the castle she must have been a very unhappy lady. Some two hundred years ago a spectre of a woman with long unkempt hair was said to be often seen wandering about the ruins.

The river Hoddnant separates Boverton from Llanilltud Fawr (Llantwit Major), a place with its known history going back to Roman times. Walking through the narrow streets, which twist and turn in all directions, you will feel that you are back in bygone days. History is written everywhere and there is evidence of antiquity in the ancient stones. The foundations of the medieval two-storeyed Town Hall date back as far as the thirteenth century. Opposite is the old Swan Inn which was once used to accommodate the Judges who held courts in the Town Hall. Before this the inn was part of the monastic college founded by St Illtud, perhaps as a place of shelter where food and alms were given to passing pilgrims.

The Royal Mint has been moved from London to Llantrisant (a place which is sometimes called 'the hole with the mint in it') but if, as is believed, coins were minted in medieval times in what is now the Swan Inn this would have been the first mint in South Wales.

On the outskirts of Llanilltud excavations in 1888 uncovered a Roman villa. An account of this important discovery by John Storries states:

> A Roman villa was uncovered in a field known locally as Caermead. No fewer than forty-one human skeletons of both sexes and all ages were found. The bodies lay in confused heaps. From the general absence of weapons, personal ornaments and similar articles, that after they were plundered they were simply left to lie where they fell. After the villa was sacked it was burnt down, and the pavement and bodies buried under debris. It has been conjectured that the massacre was perpetrated by Irish pirates in the Fifth Century.

It is possible that the first church here was also desecrated and destroyed before St Illtud founded his monastic university, a place famous before the Normans invaded Wales. The narrow streets now cover the medieval pavements over which saints have walked, and likewise in the surrounding fields are mounds covering the foundations of many ancient buildings.

St Illtud, like St David, built his sanctuary in a hollow hoping that it could not be seen by the pirates who sailed up and down the Bristol Channel. Many sought peace in this quiet place of piety and learning—Samson of Dol, Giraldus the historian, Taliesin the bard, and possibly St David. In comparison with St David's church in Pembrokeshire the present church of St Illtud is small, but its atmosphere is compelling, giving a feeling that here is a holy place—a place of peace, simplicity and charm. John Wesley, who preached there in 1777, said, 'I suppose it has been abundantly the most beautiful, as well as the most spacious parish church in Wales.'

If a place has a name, and on most maps which show the Vale of Glamorgan, Llanmihangel is printed in bold lettering, it is accepted that it is a village or at least a small hamlet. But Llanmihangel is hardly large enough to be considered a hamlet, but it is a lovely place with an old manor house and a Norman church. On a high plateau north of the church stands the fifteenth-century home of Eleanor Ddu who was drowned in a nearby pool. Whenever she was opposed, Eleanor would fly into a rage and because of her black moods she was feared as a witch. The people of the district one day seized her and fastened a metal ring on her wrist so that when possessed she could be safely tethered. On certain moonlit nights Eleanor is said to rise out of the pool and haunt the hamlet.

Ghost walking and other strange happenings occur in many villages and ancient sites in Wales; some are only legends, but others are based on fact. Two places north-east of Llanmihangel have strange stories, and one at least is substantiated. Near Colwinston is a house called Pwll-y-wrach where the baying of hounds sometimes disturbs the silence of the night. The story goes that a careless servant, off on a drunken spree, left the animals without food and water for several days. When he returned the ravenous beasts attacked and killed him.

From Colwinston several lanes run eastwards to Llanblethian, a village built on the south slope of a high ridge separating it from Cowbridge. Just below the ridge are the ruins of another castle attacked by Glyndwr. Before dealing with the castle he marched to defeat the Anglo-Norman army at Stalling Down, a moorland height above Cowbridge. During restoration of Llanblethian church a sealed crypt under the south chapel was revealed. It is said that when this underground vault was opened, three hundred male skeletons, laid in a jumbled heap one on top of another, were found. Is it possible (if the story is true) that those slain in battle at Stalling Down were brought here and, without ceremony, thrown into the crypt which was then sealed up?

Not far from the church is Cross Inn and a spot with the strange name of 'the Devil's Foot and Knee'. Both are on the western outskirts of Cowbridge–Y Dref hir yn y Waun, or 'the Long Town on the Moor'. This is an appropriate name for this town with its mile-long main street, although its coat of arms offers another reason for its name. It shows a cow standing on a bridge with a sheaf of wheat in its mouth, a reminder of the story of how a cow which entangled its horns in the balustrade of a new bridge across the River Thaw had to be slaughtered before any other beast or man could cross the bridge into the town. When a stone bridge replaced the wooden one in 1321 it was named Pont-faen which means Cowbridge.

The town has a large number of old inns and ale-houses, but it is probable that the Romans set up the first wine-houses when they made it a Roman station. Later, when the Normans surrounded the town with walls they found that the foundations of the Roman walls were a strong base on which to build. To Glyndwr the very sight of a castle or a length of walling above normal height was infuriating so he soon demolished the Norman walls, but part of the medieval walls and the south gate—Porte Mellin—can still be seen. The twelfth-century Church of the Holy Cross, mainly of Early English style, has a massive thirteenth-century embattled tower.

There is a plaque in the main street recalling the eighteenth-century stonemason and collector of manuscripts, Edward Williams, better known by his Bardic title, Iolo Morgannwg. He is buried nearby at Flemington.

5

The Glamorgan Coast

Apart from the Gower Peninsula the most picturesque stretch of the Glamorgan coastline lies between Barry and the Ogmore river. Further west the coastline is backed by an industrial belt, and not until the western end of Swansea Bay is reached is the air freshened again by the Atlantic breezes. Between Barry and Ogmore the coastline is backed by rugged cliffs, curving here and there to form small coves and bays. Above the cliffs is an upland of pastoral beauty, a green and fertile land divided by shallow valleys sheltering thatched and whitewashed cottages. This is a peaceful land, now free from the cruelty and domination of those who built the grey-towered castles.

> Not far from Caerdyff is a small island situated near the shore of the Severn, called Barri, from St Barroc who lived there, and whose remains are deposited in a chapel overgrown with ivy, having been transferred to a coffin. From hence a noble family of the maritime parts of South Wales, who owned this island and adjoining estates received the name of Barri.

So wrote the historian Giraldus whose name is associated with Barry. Many years ago the remains of St Baroc's chapel stood on Nell's Point, a promontory on the eastern side of Whitmore Bay. Centuries ago Barry Island was covered with sand dunes and would have been an uncomfortable place to live, but because of this it would have been approved by a saint wishing to find a quiet spot to build his hermitage. Baroc's island today is not so quiet, and over the site of his simple home a large holiday camp has been built, a place of jollity, 'kiss-me-quick' paper hats, candy-floss and the raucous beat of loud disco music. Another theory suggests that the hermitage stood in the centre of the island, an area now covered by a large fairground.

All along the coast there are strange tales of pirates, smugglers and ghostly visitations. Sully Island, to the east of Sully Bay, is said to be haunted by the ghosts of Roman soldiers and Irish and Danish pirates. There could be some truth in this story, for about a hundred years ago a large number of Roman coins were dug up.

On the mainland, opposite the island, are the ruins of Sully House which were once haunted by a spectre of a woman garbed in funereal black. This haunting is connected with the story of a local sea-captain whose wife died at sea. Being afraid to disturb his superstitious crew he made plausible excuses for her non-appearance, and placed the corpse in a chest for burial at home. For some reason there was delay in getting a coffin so he buried the chest in the garden, intending, as soon as possible, to arrange for a formal burial and service. When he went to dig it up the chest had gone so he assumed that someone, seeing him bury it and believing that the chest contained treasure, had stolen it. Soon afterwards the ghost of his wife, weeping and wailing, was seen walking about the garden. The sight of this black apparition terrified the local people who would not pass the house after dark. This went on for many years until workmen repairing a nearby property found a female skeleton under a large paving stone. After the bones had been laid to rest in a Christian churchyard the ghost ceased to walk. A strange story, but one that has persisted for years.

The old Celtic saints must have loved this part of Wales, and considered it a convenient place to welcome their brothers from across the Irish Sea. Not all who landed here from Ireland came to pray, for many came to plunder and pillage. About two miles west of Barry is Porthkerry where St Curig built a church, and the porth (port) linked its name with Ceri, a Welsh chieftain. There is a 225-acre country park at Porthkerry, an unspoilt valley through which runs an impressive railway viaduct that was built to transport coal to the docks. On the edge of the cliffs are the Bulwarks, ancient fortifications overlooking the Bristol Channel, and possibly representing the first Norman invasion of Wales from the sea. Not only Irish pirates landed here; the Vikings came from across the northern seas and built settlements on two small islands known as the Flat Holm and Steep Holm in the middle of the channel. Saints and murderers are linked with these islands—Gildas, the monk-historian, lived there for a time, and it is said that two of the barons who murdered Thomas à Becket were buried on one of them.

Further west along the coast is Aberthaw with its picturesque fourteenth-century inn. With its walls from 2ft to 7ft thick the Blue Anchor Inn was built to withstand the severest storm and tempest. When ships returned from the West Indies with rich cargoes of tobacco, rum and sugar many an illicit deal was probably made with the landlord of the inn. There are records that the old port of Aberthaw received cargo-carrying ships in Norman days, and before then local people drove Saxon invaders back to their galleys along a route known for centuries as 'the Robbers Run'. In about 1030 a battle took place along the 'run' and when, about a hundred years later, the ground was excavated for constructional foundations to be laid, a large number of skeletons with broken skulls were found.

Beyond Aberthaw the cliffs are lined with prehistoric tumuli and encampments. One of the largest is Castle Ditches with ramparts overlooking the sea and the Col-huw river valley. When St Illtud

The picturesque Blue Anchor Inn at Aberthaw dates from the fourteenth century and is a favourite place of refreshment for local people and tourists along the coast of the Bristol Channel. Records suggest that the inn was a busy place in the days when Aberthaw was one of the most important ports along the coast of southern Wales

came across the sea to build his church at Llanilltud Fawr (Llantwit Major) he may have landed at Col-huw Point. It has been established that a port existed here in the fourteenth century, and some claim that it was in use by the Romans. Smeaton used limestone from Aberthaw in the building of Eddystone Lighthouse between 1756 and 1759.

Continuing westward, the next point of interest is Tresilian Bay where a cave is supposed to have given entry to a secret passage through the cliffs to St Donat's Castle. Secret passages from caves and historic houses are often romantic but not always factual, but here fact has overtaken fiction. For reasons which can only be assumed as romantic the parents of General Picton were married in this cave. Perhaps it was a runaway marriage and this cave was nearer than Gretna Green.

St Donat's Castle is claimed to have been continually occupied since the early part of the fourteenth century, and it may have been erected on the site of an Early Iron Age fort. Many of its owners had a special hatred of pirates, one of them building a high watchtower from which he could check any suspicious activities in the channel or along the foreshore beneath the cliffs. About 1297 Sir Peter Stradling became established at the castle. His father, Sir Henry Stradling, had once been captured and held to ransom by a pirate called Colyn Dolphyn. He was revenged by his son when Sir Peter captured Dolphyn after his ship was wrecked on the coast near the castle. One story relates that the sea-brigand was hanged in the castle gardens; another version tells that he was buried up to his neck in the sands and left to die at high tide.

The Stradling family fought bravely on the side of the Royalist army at the Battle of St Fagan's in May 1648, but when Sir Thomas Stradling was killed in a duel at Montpellier in France in 1738 the line came to an end. After the Civil War, although still inhabited the castle was neglected until the American newspaper magnate William Randolph Hearst bought and restored it. The restorative work was extensive, and on the site of a medieval jousting ground he built the inevitable swimming pool. Today the castle is known as the first international sixth-form school in the world. It is called Atlantic College and is large enough to accommodate three hundred boys and girls from over forty countries.

The local church is of interest, dating from the eleventh century and containing memorials to the Stradling family, including some curious sixteenth-century paintings. A medieval cross stands in the churchyard and nearby is a fifteenth-century look-out tower.

Nash Point is further west along the coast where two small lighthouses give warning of treacherous reefs and rocks. Between Nash Point and Dunraven Bay the cliffs are topped with several prehistoric encampments and settlements, and in a wooded hollow once stood Dunraven Castle. In comparison St Donat's is modern, for a fortress stood here long before the Normans fought and won a battle at Hastings. If Bran, the father of Caractacus, did live here the foundations of the castle must have been very old. The castle was pulled down some years ago, but as it played an important part in the history of the Glamorganshire coastline it seems worthy of a mention.

The coast at this point faces a treacherous and dangerous stretch of water, as evidenced by the numerous memorial stones in churchyards along the coast marking the burial of shipwrecked mariners. At Monknash is a stone to the memory of the crew of the *Malleny*, lost on the Tusker Rock on 15 October 1886. The Tusker Rock is a dangerous reef about a mile out to sea off Ogmore.

The foundations of Dunraven Castle are to be found on a headland overlooking Southerndown Bay. From this pleasant bay a road hugs the coast to Ogmore-by-Sea, one of the favourite holiday places along the north coast of the Bristol Channel. The Ogmore river turns the road northwards to the site of another grim Norman fortress overlooking the confluence of the Ogmore and Ewenny rivers. William de Londres ordered his masons to build a keep which is said to have the oldest Norman stonework in the county. But were these stones laid before the ones forming a causeway across the river? Were the stones set in the bed of the shallow river by prehistoric people? One legend refers to them as St Teilo's Steps, while another tale relates that the stones were laid so that an admirer of one of the de Londres ladies could visit her without wetting his feet.

Religious houses were often built by powerful lords and chieftains, English and Welsh (or Anglo-Norman and Welsh), as tangible evidence of genuine penance and a new-found state of piety. It is thought that a priory a short distance away at Ewenny was built by de Londres to obtain absolution from the Church after he had murdered a pious man who had come to plead with him to lead a better life. The de Londres women must have been kinder, for when a man caught poaching was sentenced to death by Morice de Londres, the Norman's daughter pleaded with her father for clemency; as it was her birthday her petition was granted.

From the stepping stones across the river a path goes through a leafy byway to the village of Merthyr Mawr, a picture-postcard village with well-maintained thatched cottages set amid the trees. The Ogmore river here is spanned by two bridges. One is modern, while the other is a four-arched medieval bridge which has two apertures traditionally used by farmers who pushed in their sheep to wash them at sheep-dipping time. Near the latter bridge a notorious inn once stood, kept by an unsavoury character known as Cap Goch (Red Cap) because he always wore a red cap. A gruesome story relates that in 1870 when the inn was pulled down a smugglers' hoard was discovered, and partly-decomposed bodies were uncovered in the garden. Some folk claim that the ghost of Shoni of the Red Cap still haunts the roads near the bridge, inviting travellers to spend the night at an inn which no longer exists.

Merthyr Mawr House stands downstream where there is a ruined oratory—St Rogue's Chapel. Kept in the grounds is a collection of stones found in the area. Two are inscribed and are known as the Conbelanus Cross and the Dobilaucus Cross or Goblin Stone.

A lane runs through the trees to Merthyr Mawr Warren, a large area of sand dunes between the woods and the sea. On the edge of the dunes, almost buried in the sand, are the remains of Candleston Castle, a fifteenth-century manor house, so ruined and derelict that it is difficult to believe that people lived here less than a century ago.

The wind-blown sands of the warren are continually shifting, and as they cover some ancient settlements, so they reveal others. On one occasion they uncovered a large tumulus where six skeletons of the Beaker Age were found, and here and there archaeologists have collected prehistoric implements and weapons last used in the Bronze and Iron Ages.

A walk across the sands on a hot and windless day will give a very good idea of what an uncomfortable place the Sahara Desert is, and if you should suddenly find yourself in the middle of an Arabian cavalry charge, or catch sight of parched and exhausted soldiers stumbling through the dunes, do not think that by some strange warp of time you have been taken to another place and age, for this is a favourite location of film-makers for the enactment of desert scenes. A film entitled *Seven Graves to Cairo* was made here, and the desert scenes were very convincing.

The words 'swan' and 'sea' have nothing to do with the naming of this Welsh coastal town. The long curving bay between Swansea and Mumbles Head was an easy place after a long sea voyage for the Scandinavian pirates to make a landing, and the uplands beyond the western end of the bay a suitable place to establish forts and settlements. In winter it was also warmer than the cold fiords and mountains of their Nordic homeland. So when the Danish rover Sweyn anchored his wooden ships in the bay, he was pleased to have his ownership established when his warriors called it Sweyn's Eye. When a town grew up along the eastern shore of the bay, the name Swansea was a logical corruption.

The local tribes put up a fierce resistance to the occupation of their land by these Nordic pirates, and were enraged when their cattle were stolen, their womenfolk ravished and their homes set on fire. There are many stories and legends of their battles and attempts to storm the hill forts of the invaders. However, soon after the Normans landed at Hastings they found they were faced with more formidable foes.

The Welsh failed to throw the Normans out of the castle they built at Swansea, but had better luck in taking their fortresses in the Gower Peninsula. Owain Glyndwr eventually completed the destruction of Swansea Castle. What little is left are but fragments of a fortified home built by Henry Gower, Bishop of St David's (c1340) on the site and foundations of the castle.

Apart from being an attractive seaside town, or at least that part fronting Swansea Bay, the town and the district around have always had a variety of industries. In the reign of Queen Elizabeth I coal was mined, and according to a writer of this time the coal was brought out of the ground by

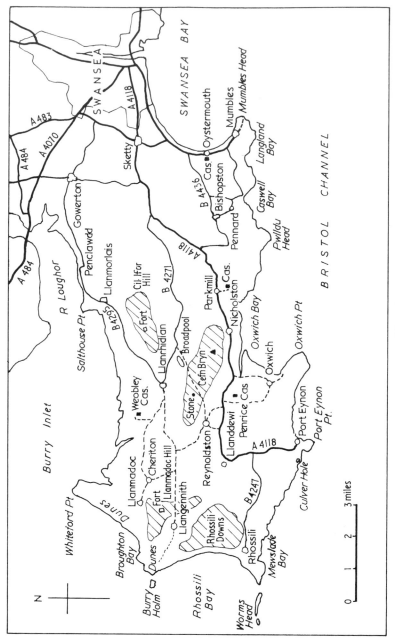

Map 6

using hot engines for lifting the coal out of the pit, but people carried the coal up the slope and on stayers along their backs, whereas they now sink their pit down right four square and with a wynlas turned by four men, they drew up coal, a barrel full at once by a rope.

For many years coal was the main export, and suitable methods of transportation (other than by panniers carried by packhorse and mule) from mines to dock had to be introduced. When waggons were used it was complained that the noise they made passing through the streets was unbearable—but much worse than this, the vibration curdled beer brewing in the cellars of the town. In about 1720, Swansea became known for its production of fine straw hats; about the same time manufacture of the finest porcelain commenced, an industry which continued until the middle of the nineteenth century.

The poet and writer Dylan Thomas (1914–53) was born in a hillside villa overlooking the sea. He did not have a high opinion of his birthplace for he described it as being an 'ugly lovely town'. In another part of the town Richard (Beau) Nash was born in 1674; what would he and Dylan have thought of each other? The elegant Beau and, as he described himself, the snub-nosed Dylan with his pork-pie hat, chequered overcoat and 'conscious woodbine'. They would have been an odd pair, and what would they have talked about had they met in the old Kardomah coffee house? Beau Nash became famous for his promotion of Bath as a city of high culture and art. The spa waters must certainly have agreed with him, far more than the alcoholic beverages of Dylan, for after living in Bath for fifty years he died in 1761 at the ripe old age of eighty-seven.

For three nights in February 1941 German bombers poured their loads of high-explosive and incendiary bombs over Swansea, reducing its centre to rubble. Now, like London, it has its own Oxford Street together with other new streets with colourful gardens and large department stores. The town was always known for its splendid market; now it has an even better one with a glass roof spanning 190ft. Commercial Swansea is built between a long coastal strip and the bottom of gently sloping hills rising to an area appropriately called The Uplands. The town is laid out in an orderly pattern. Alongside the bay is the holidaymakers' seaside; behind, and within easy reach, is the new shopping centre, theatres and civic buildings, while overlooking the town and seafront is residential Swansea. The upland area has its own shops where the service, after the brashness of the lower town, is quiet, courteous and personal.

Before the days of easy travel Swansea Bay, with its long stretch of fine golden sands, was one of the most popular holiday resorts along the coast. A railway ran along the curve of the bay taking visitors to other pleasant places such as Oystermouth, Mumbles and, within easy distance, the smaller bays of Bracelet, Langland and Caswell. The Swansea to Mumbles Railway was the first in the United Kingdom to be used for passengers. In 1806 it was an industrial tramroad drawn by horses, then from 1877 it was powered by steam until 1929 when it was converted to electricity. It finally closed to passengers in 1960.

The motor car made travelling easier so in time Swansea, as a popular seaside resort, became second to the peninsula of Gower and was referred to as its Gateway.

A few miles west along Swansea Bay (on the A4067) is Black Pill where a turning past a pseudo-Roman bridge is the direct route over Clyne Common into the peninsula. Like most of the classified Gower highways the road is well surfaced but very narrow. Pennard Castle, half a mile south of Parkmill, is worth a visit— impressive remains dating from the late thirteenth century. Just after passing the weathered grey towers of Penrice Castle a lane on the right goes to Reynoldston, a small village at the foot of Cefn Bryn. With cottages grouped around the green it is a charming village, and being situated in the centre of the peninsula it is a convenient centre for making daily explorations. Overlooking the green is the King Arthur Inn, a comfortable place to stay. There is a Victorian church built on the site of an earlier one which contains some interesting monuments and registers.

From Reynoldston it is an easy walk to the 600ft summit of Cefn Bryn and the great stone from which the village inn takes its name. The kingly Arthur seems to have scattered memorials to per- petuate his memory in every part of Britain. There must be as many of these stones of Arthur as the canopied four-posters which offered a good night's rest to Queen Elizabeth I. This particular stone, according to an old legend, was an irritating pebble cast by Arthur from his sandal. If this is true, the greatness of his deeds could only have been equalled by his stature. The 25-ton boulder once formed a capstone to a prehistoric burial chamber and legend has it that the stone takes an annual trip down to the sea for a drink each New Year's Eve. But if the tourist has little interest in such Neolithic remains, the view from the top of Cefn Bryn will compensate him for his efforts, particularly in the late evening when the setting sun, sinking slowly behind the ancient Danish earthworks on Llanmadoc Hill, adds a strange after-glow to accentuate the mystery of these man-made contours. If the day is clear, both coastlines of the peninsula are visible as are, across the southern channel, the isle of Lundy and the coast of Somerset and North Devon.

A switchback road snakes its way down the north side of Cefn Bryn, turning westward at Broad Pool (a pond rich in aquatic flora and fauna) through central Gower to the village of Llanrhidian, near which are the extensive Llanrhidian salt marshes. The parish church has a strange carved limestone block in its porch which may date from the ninth century. On the village green is a large standing stone with rusted iron staples embedded in its sides; this was once the local pillory and whipping post. Overlooking, and casting a dark shadow over the spot of miserable penance, is the mass of Cil lfor Hill on which are the massive ramparts of an Early Iron Age fort covering some eight acres.

Four miles away, north-eastwards along the B4295, is Penclawd, a village on the bleak north coast known for its cockle industry. At certain times of the day, according to the tidal flow, the hardy cockle-women can be seen leading their heavily laden donkeys from the sands. The area was once an artillery and bombing range so care should be taken to keep to the main paths if exploring the country here.

From Llanrhidian a pleasant cliff-top walk leads to the most picturesque of all the Gower castles. However exasperating the sight of Weobley Castle must have been to its Welsh assailants, it will not fail to fire the imagination of the visitor seeing it for the first time. Built in the thirteenth and fourteenth centuries by Henry Beaufort, Earl of Warwick, to protect the north coast of the peninsula, it is a fortified house rather than a castle. There is no place for a garrison and the rooms are domestic. Porch rooms added in the fifteenth century have become a farmhouse.

The towers of Weobley Castle stand high above the marshlands of Llanrhidian and the Burry Inlet. The sight of these strong Norman towers must have exasperated the Welsh assailants, who probably cursed the impregnability of the castle walls (*Wales Tourist Board*)

Many roads lead from Reynoldston. One goes south to Port Eynon, the prettiest of all the Gower villages. Not far away from the old Ship Inn, with its unusual port-hole windows, are the haunted ruins of Salt House. This was once the headquarters of John Lucas and his gang of smugglers, a wild bunch of men who engineered many wrecks along this coast during the sixteenth century. It is possible that the small bays and coves along the coast take their names from the activities of the smugglers. There is Pwll Du (Black Pool), Brandy Cove, which needs no explanation, and Port Eynon—named after Eynon who was a friend of John Lucas. Around Port Eynon Point is Culver Hole, a cleft in the rocks closed with dressed masonry pierced with apertures to give light and access to the interior. The true purpose of this man-made cave is uncertain. Was it used by John Lucas as his store, and was there once a passage from it to Salt House? The word 'culver' is interesting for it might be a corruption of *culfre*, an old English word for pigeon. A similar word for a wood-pigeon is still used in certain parts of Britain, so it might well have been a pigeon-house for nesting holes can be seen in the interior. In a corner of the local graveyard there is a carved marble figure of a lifeboatman. This is a memorial to three crew members of the local lifeboat who were drowned in the course of their duties in January 1916.

Because of its exposed position, one should visit Rhossili on a warm and windless day, for the long sweep of the bay offers no protection from even the lightest Atlantic breeze. Built on the edge of 300ft cliffs, this must surely be the most exposed hamlet in the world. Reaching out to sea below the cliffs is a narrow rocky headland shaped like the head of a worm. The Scandinavian word for a serpent is *orme* so the modern name of Worm's Head is apt. At low tide it is possible to walk to the head of the worm, but be sure to allow sufficient time to return to the mainland. The golden sands of this picturesque bay cover many an engineered wreck. In the seventeenth century a Spanish ship ran aground above high watermark and its treasure, mostly Spanish dollars and pieces of eight,

The Worms Head, Rhossili. The Scandinavian invaders of Gower would have called the rocky headland an Orme, their word for serpent, so its modern name is a suitable one. The golden sands of Rhossili Bay cover many wrecks, most of them engineered by those who had little concern for the safety of others. In the seventeenth century they contrived to lure a Spanish treasure ship to run aground

were taken from the wrecked ship by a Mr Mansel who fled the country with his loot. In 1807 and in 1833 the wreck, uncovered by the tide, was sighted; coins dated 1625 were found on both occasions, but the wreck has never been seen again. At the north end of the bay is Burry Holm, a small islet infested by rabbits and providing a sanctuary for sea-birds. Very little of the Gower Peninsula is without interest, for even on this storm-lashed isle there are traces of an Iron Age fort and the scant ruins of an Early Christian chapel.

North-west of Reynoldston are two of the most attractive of the Gower churches; these are at Cheriton and Llanmadoc. Those interested in fine woodcarving will find in Cheriton hand-carved sanctuary rails and a matching altar front, exquisitely fashioned by John Davies, a former priest of this parish. The Early English church at Llanmadoc was restored in 1865. It has a saddleback roof with stepped gables and a small tower. Built into a window-sill is a Celtic gravestone bearing a Latin inscription. The altar front here was also carved by John Davies. From Llanmadoc a steep narrow lane runs over the Bulwark, an Iron Age fort, between Llanmadoc Hill and Ryder's Down to Llangennith. This place was the home of St Cenydd, a grandson of Dichocus, a prince of Brittany. Inside the Norman church is a mutilated effigy of De la Mere, one of the lords of Gower. Some folk refer to this effigy as being the 'Dolly Mare' of Llangennith.

The Gower Peninsula holds much attraction: the roads and lanes winding their way through undulating countryside, the scenic beauty of the lovely bays and coves and exhilarating heights with sweet-scented moors. There are so many places to visit—the sunlit bays of Pobbles, Three Cliffs and Oxwich; the prehistoric bone caves and the haunts of smugglers; the grey Norman castles and the primitive fortresses of even greater age, all offering numerous links with the past.

6

West to Carmarthen and St David's Head

The first chapter told of a journey from the eastern border of Gwent to a Roman fort on the lonely moorlands of Mynydd-bach Trecastle. From the village of Trecastle the road runs westward to Llandovery, an important junction with a past going back to Roman and Norman times. The Welsh name for Llandovery is Llanymddfai, 'The Church between Two Rivers', a strategic position recognised by the Romans who built there their fort of Loventium. A Christian church stands in the centre of the fort, its external walls having narrow sections of Roman brickwork, the ruins of an early twelfth-century castle indicating its later Norman ownership. The church was restored in 1915 by W. D. Caroe and he salvaged the structure rather than rebuilt it.

Llandovery has a college, and in the chapel is a painting of the Crucifixion by Graham Sutherland. Two authors found the town an agreeable and useful place. George Borrow described it as 'a small beautiful town situated amidst fertile meadows', and Lady Charlotte Guest must have made many visits to the local printers who set up presses to produce her translation, from old Welsh, of the *Mabinogion*. The *Mabinogion* was her name for a collection of eleven anonymous tales, taken from oral stories which date from the second half of the eleventh century to the close of the thirteenth century. Two original MSS survive: the White Book of Rhydderch (1300–25), now in the National Library of Wales, and the Red Book of Hergest (1375–1425), now in the library of Jesus College, Oxford.

The town, situated at the southern end of the Tywi valley, was an assembling point for cattle to be driven along the drovers' mountain roads to Welsh and English markets. The drovers had their own bank, known as the Bank of the Black Ox until it was taken over by Lloyds in 1909.

89

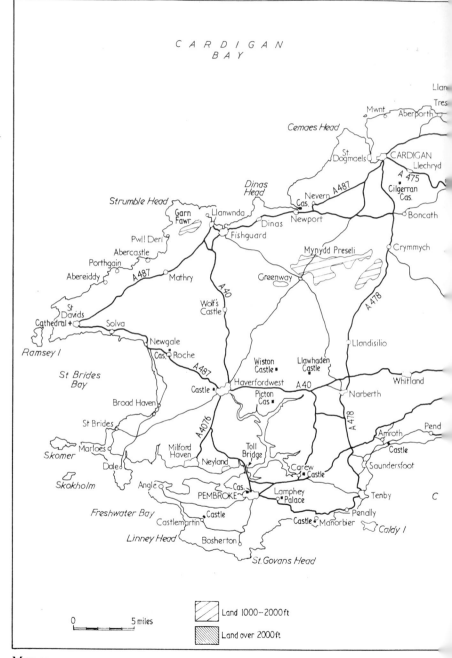

CARDIGAN
BAY

Llan
Tres
Mwnt Aberporth
Cemaes Head
St. CARDIGAN
Dogmaels Llechryd
A 475
Dinas Cilgerran
Head Cas.
Strumble Head Nevern A487
Garn Llanwnda Cas. Boncath
Fawr Dinas Newport
Pwll Deri Fishguard Crymmych
Abercastle Mynydd Preseli
Porthgain
Abereiddy A487 Mathry Greenway A 478
St Wolf's
Davids Castle
Cathedral + Solva Llandisilio
Ramsey I Newgale Whitland
Cas. Roche Wiston Llawhaden
St Brides A487 Castle Castle
Bay Castle Haverfordwest A40 Narberth
Picton
Broad Haven Cas.
St Brides Pend
Skomer A4076 Amroth
Marloes Milford Toll Castle
Dale Haven Bridge Saundersfoot
Skokholm Neyland Carew
Angle Cas. Castle Tenby C
PEMBROKE Lamphey
Freshwater Bay Castle Palace Penally
Castlemartin Castle Manorbier Caldy I
Linney Head Bosherton
St. Govans Head

0   5 miles

Land 1000–2000 ft

Land over 2000 ft

Map 7

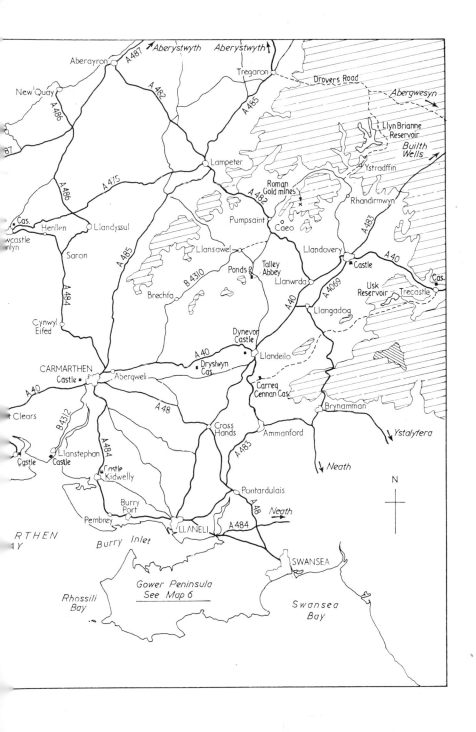

About four miles away a turning south-west of the main road goes through Llangadog over the mountains to the Swansea valley and the industrial south. Just outside Llangadog is Castell Meurig, an early mound probably named after a local Welsh chieftain. When the valley road reaches Pontarllechau, and the Three Horseshoes pub, a minor road on the right leads to a complexity of lanes running to many interesting places; above the village of Bethlehem is the Iron Age fort of Carn Goch or, as named on some maps, Y Gaer Fawr, which means 'The Great Fort'. As it is one of the largest prehistoric forts in Wales, still having 20ft ramparts on its western side, the latter name is more suitable. It is almost half a mile in length, and even after two thousand years of wear and weather it is still possible to trace the line of its ramparts and ditches.

From Bethlehem, lanes climb over the hills before going down to the Cennen river valley overlooked and guarded by the ruined castle of Carreg Cennen. Approached from any direction, and in all conditions of light and weather, the first sight of the castle is formidable and magical. Standing on a crag 300ft above the river valley, one feels that it is a haunted place and a home for black ravens and falcons. A fortress of some kind stood on this eagles' crag before Roman and Norman times, and it was not until the dawn of the thirteenth century that Lord Rhys ap Gruffydd built towers and curtain walls strong enough to withstand any assault. The finding of coins of the first and fourth centuries offered proof that the Romans had made use of this impregnable site, and when a passage through the rock to a cave was explored evidence of prehistoric occupation was found. After excavating through a layer of stalagmites the remains of two adults and two children were found, and near them portions of a primitive necklace. During the years following the Wars of the Roses outlaws and bandits made the castle their headquarters. These lawless gangs terrorised the neighbourhood until a concerted attack, led by the sheriff of Carmarthen, captured the castle and drove them away.

From Carreg Cennen a lane soon joins the main road at Llandeilo, a place taking its name from the *llan* which St Teilo founded. It is claimed that the saint was buried here, but as two other places in Wales make the same claim there is some confusion. True to saintly form St Teilo made sure that his name would be remembered by blessing a well whose water would cure consumption, as long as the sufferer drank from the hollowed skull of the saint.

A short distance west of Llandeilo are two other interesting castles; Dynevor and Dryslwyn. The present castle at Dynevor is modern. The first, ninth-century, castle was owned by Roderick, a prince claiming sovereignty over all Wales. In later years the Normans, as they usually did, took over the site and built on it a stone stronghold. Spenser writes of Merlin's cave being 'among the woody hills of Dynevowre'. The old Welsh wizard seems to have owned as many residential caves as his protégé Arthur. Dryslwyn, a picturesque ruin, stands on the site of an Iron Age fort.

From Llandeilo a road winds its way northwards through rich pasture and woodland to the twin lakes of Talley, lakes which must have supplied the monks of the nearby twelfth-century abbey with abundant water and piscatorial delicacies. Years ago Talley had a longer and more descriptive name: Tal-y-Llychan, 'Head of the Lakes'. The ecclesiastical builders invariably found beautiful sites, and here the ruins of Talley Abbey, surrounded by attractive dwellings and farm buildings, nestle in a delectable hollow. In 1215 one of the abbots was appointed Bishop of St David's. Just north of the ruins a lane follows the Cothi river north to Caio and Pumpsaint.

The Romans came to a spot between Caio and Pumpsaint to mine for gold. Traces of their mines can still be seen, and in places a rock-cut aqueduct which brought water to the workings is still traceable. Gold coins and ornaments have been found at this Welsh Klondike—a golden torque, armlets and other Roman jewels can be seen in the British Museum. Not one, but five Celtic saints favoured this spot below the Cambrian mountains, so it was feasible to name the village Pumpsaint, which is Welsh for 'five saints'.

Having travelled this far from Llandeilo a journey through one of the most beautiful valleys in Wales should not be missed. The distance is only about ten miles, but every mile is one of sheer delight. The road, following the Cothi river, runs along a narrow ledge carved out of Mynydd Mallaen. Through the trees are glimpses of the dancing musical Cothi, sometimes placid and then

Talley is a shortened version of the Welsh Talyllychau which means 'Head of the Lakes'. The ruined abbey is beautifully set amid the hills between Llandeilo and Lampeter. It was originally founded by Rhys ap Gruffydd, and is the only one in Wales built by the Premonstratensians, a similar order to the Cistercians. Near the abbey are two small lakes (*Wales Tourist Board*)

suddenly turbulent as it cascades over rocky falls. The road ends at the hamlet of Nantybai, crossing the river to wind northwards through Ystradffin and on to Llyn Brianne, a reservoir which was opened in 1972. The waters of the reservoir are held back by an enormous dam, and the contractors' constructional roads have been graded and surfaced so that it is possible for the motorist to enjoy a scenic run around the most beautiful man-made lake in Wales. From the northern end of the lake it is possible to drive across the moors to the old drovers' road between Tregaron and Abergwesyn. After exploring the Llyn Brianne reservoir a good map will indicate several interesting routes back to Llandeilo.

The next important point west is Carmarthen, the Roman seafort which they called Meridunum. There is little to remind one today that it was once an important junction in their system of military roads. Its castle was a home for many princes of South Wales, but when it fell into Norman hands Glyndwr captured and burnt it down.

Many famous names are connected with the town. Merlin is supposed to have been born there, and when the Welsh bowmen fought at Agincourt, the sign of Merlin was the emblem of the Carmarthen men. In St Peter's Church there is a monument to Robert Ferrar, the Protestant Bishop of St David's who ended his days as a martyr when he was burnt alive in the market place in 1555. It also contains the tomb of Sir Rhys-ap-Thomas and his wife. Sir Rhys did much to help Henry Tudor win the English throne. In more recent years there are memories of those who fought against the injustice of the turnpike gates, particularly those who were caught and transported. These men of the district, disguised as women, were known as 'The daughters of Rebecca'. This title was an apt and imaginative use of a Biblical prophecy which proclaimed that 'Rebecca's seed should possess the gates of those which hate them.' In 1843 hundreds of the 'daughters' swept through the countryside tearing down and burning the hated tollgates. Carmarthen is the only Welsh town having the honour of a sword being carried before its mayor on state occasions, a right granted in 1546 by Henry VIII. The sword which is now used was presented to the town in about 1564.

South of Carmarthen, at Kidwelly, off the B4312, overlooking the Tywi estuary and the coastal lowlands, stands a large moated castle, a fortress almost as large as Caerphilly and Pembroke castles. The Normans were hated by all in this area, and few opportunities were missed to oppose them. As she was unable to await the return of her husband, Rhys-ap-Tudor, who was at war in another part of Wales, his wife Gwenllian led her troops against the Normans. The Welsh were defeated and Gwenllian was captured and beheaded on the field of battle. One moonlit night a villager met her ghost searching the battlefield for her missing head. Although very afraid, he searched with her for several nights until he found it, where it had been flung, in the midst of a thorn bush. After recovering her head, Gwenllian was never seen again. A nearby field is still known as Maes Gwenllian in memory of this brave woman.

From St Clears, about nine miles west of Carmarthen along the A40, there is a choice of routes: the A40 trunk road to Haverfordwest; the A477 to Pembroke; or a third route the A4066 for exploration of the southern coast. Laugharne, if the latter route is selected, is the first place of interest. It is a small village of fishermen's cottages, period houses and a ruined castle on the edge of an estuary. Walk along the river bank at the right time of year and you might see the ghost of a past owner of the castle floating through the swirling mist towards you in a coracle. General Laugharne appears once a year, completely naked, baling out his coracle with a cocked hat. In the village the name of a restaurant is a reminder that the Welsh poet Dylan Thomas lived here, and many stories of his unconventional ways are still told in the local pubs where he was a regular customer. Dylan lived in several houses until settling down at the Boat House where he wrote his most famous work, *Under Milk Wood*.

From the estuary there is a long westward stretch of fine hard sand as far as Pendine, a place used during the 1920s for attacks on the world land speed record. Sir Malcolm Campbell pushed his Bluebird to 146mph in September 1924. The same year, the Welsh driver J. G. Parry-Thomas was decapitated by the broken driving chain of his car, the car being buried in the dunes. In 1969 it was dug up by an enthusiast and expertly restored.

Further west along the coast is Amroth Castle which once offered hospitality to Lord Nelson and his beloved Emma.

Thousands of years ago the foreshore fronting the castle extended further into Carmarthen Bay, and when the tide is exceptionally low traces of a sunken forest are uncovered. At one time the skeleton of a pig, with an arrow-head embedded in its vertebrae, was found in the roots of a tree. Scientific tests dated the find to be about 10,000 years old.

The coastline from here as far as Saundersfoot was used in 1943 for a full-scale rehearsal of the D-Day assault on Normandy. The beaches swarmed with troops, guns, tanks and landing craft, and Sir Winston Churchill came to watch the proceedings from an inn at Wisemans Bridge. Not many years ago Saundersfoot was a quiet place for a restful holiday, but now the bay is dominated by self-service cafés, gift shops, and garish places lined with one-armed-bandit machines which stand side by side with bingo and disco halls.

Around Monkstone Point is Tenby, one of the most attractive seaside towns in Wales, but as it is in 'Little England beyond Wales' the honours must be shared. Henry I and Henry II saw it expedient to dilute the Welshness of this part of their kingdom, so when in the twelfth century the Low Countries were severely flooded they invited the Flemish to make a new home in south Pembrokeshire. Henry II, seeking further security and military help, organised a second migration, selecting those who were skilled in the martial arts.

Tenby has played its part in the history of our land. An Earl of Pembroke strengthened the walls of the town and the castle in 1457, and in later years Queen Elizabeth I sent her masons to further improve the defences. Thomas White, a less illustrious person, hid the teenage Henry Tudor after the Battle of Tewkesbury until the future king was able to sail from Tenby to France. After Bosworth Thomas was rewarded for his loyal help with a gift of land.

The area south of the A477, between St Clears and Pembroke Dock and the inland waters of Milford Haven, is a peninsula of similar shape to the Gower. It contains some of the most interesting places in Pembrokeshire. Just a short distance beyond Castle Headland the towers of Manorbier Castle overlook a secluded sandy bay. In 1146, this castle was the birthplace of Giraldus Cambrensis, son of Princess Angharad who was the daughter of Nêst, a lady who was generally referred to as 'the Helen of Wales' because her beauty is said to have equalled that of Helen of Troy. Nêst, once the mistress of Henry I, was always ready to favour any knight reckless and bold enough to take her to his castle. The lovely lady had numerous admirers who found her less virtuous than lovely.

Westwards is Bosherston, where there are three streams blocked by sandbars forming the Bosherston Pools, extensive lakes covered with water-lilies. This picturesque spot gave credence to the story that King Arthur came here to die after returning the magic sword Excalibur to the spirit of the lake. From here one can drive to a headland named after St Govan who built a small chapel in a cleft between the cliffs. Below the chapel the sea crashes over great rocks, foaming and swirling through arched buttresses of rock fashioned by nature to support the precipitous cliffs. The identity of the saintly Govan is shrouded in mystery. Some insist that he was Sir Gawain; others, because of a similarity of name, claim that he was an Irish monk named Gobham. To the west of Bosherston is another fissure in the cliffs known as 'Huntsman's Leap', so named because a huntsman died of fright after seeing the extent of the drop over which his mount had jumped.

Later clerical gentlemen, forsaking the 'sackcloth and ashes' way of life, sought more comfortable quarters than the early saints. Not for them the discomfort of island-sited and seawashed hermitages exposed to all winds and weather. At Lamphey, just east of Pembroke, the medieval bishops built themselves a comfortable palace with fishponds, orchards and fine gardens. Work commenced on the Palace about the middle of the thirteenth century, and although not as large or as grand as the palace at St David's it must have been a splendid home, for in the sixteenth century it was still attractive enough to be the birthplace and home of Robert Devereaux, Queen Elizabeth I's favourite. Although now a ruin, with its three great halls and a chapel it is still impressive.

The area south between Bosherston and Castlemartin, because of its use for military training in armoured warfare, is often closed, but access to Castlemartin is usually possible from the B4319 road. Due to these military activities little of the village is now attractive, but it will always be remembered because its name was given to a fine breed of long-horned cattle. The road now goes on to

Freshwater, a two-mile-long bay exposed to the full force of south-westerly storms. The village, and the more sheltered bay of Angle, is north of Freshwater Bay. It is a small seaside holiday place made attractive by colourwashed houses and pretty gardens.

Pembroke is on the north side of the peninsula and the road (B4326) to this historic town runs along a high ridge with magnificent views to north and south. All along this old ridgeway are traces of early civilisation; near Orielton is a cromlech called the 'Devil's Quoit', and in a nearby field excavations revealed a Bronze Age burial site where were found the bones of a man with a bronze dagger at his side.

From all approaches Pembroke is dominated by the exceptionally high Norman keep built in 1199 by William Marshall, Earl of Pembroke. The general layout of the town is of one wide street leading to the great castle on a rock platform between two inlets, or

Pembroke Castle, one of the strongest in West Wales, was founded in 1090, and in later years it was the birthplace of Henry Tudor, the Welsh nobleman who wrested the crown of England from Richard III at the Battle of Bosworth (*Wales Tourist Board*)

pwlls, of the Milford Haven. The Normans fought hard to reach Pembroke, and after they had defeated Rhys ap Tewdwr they began to fortify the riverside site with the usual protective wooden palisade. Henry I appointed Gerald de Windsor, who had set about replacing the temporary fort with a stone castle, as official custodian. The wily Gerald, seeking peace and time to further his advancement, married Nêst the daughter of Rhys ap Tewdwr, conveniently ignoring the fact that she came straight from King Henry's bed, bringing with her his bastard son. The King wished to be rid of her; Gerald sought further royal favour; Nêst's ambitions were as strong as her ingrained sensuality—so the arrangement was satisfactory to all.

Apart from its domination of the town the strength and impregnability of the tall Norman keep dictated the history of Pembroke for centuries. It resisted attacks from Prince Llywelyn the Great and Owain Glyndwr and, in 1648, Cromwell's siege guns failed to inflict much damage on it. In 1457 Henry Tudor was born in one of the castle towers, living in Pembroke until 1471 when events forced him to sail from Tenby to Brittany, returning in 1485 to take the English crown from Richard III at Bosworth. During World War II the town was uncomfortably close to the docks which suffered from constant attack by German bombers. As a military target it was of prime importance to the enemy, and when the great oil storage tanks were set alight in 1940 the town and dockyard were lit up for three weeks!

East of Pembroke on the bank of the Cleddau river are the ruins of Carew Castle, another castle which came into the hands of Gerald de Windsor when he married Nêst. The earliest part of the fortress, with its high curtain walls and massive drum towers, reflects the war-torn days of its early years of occupation, but when the castle fell into the hands of Sir Rhys ap Thomas he added a Great Hall with wide mullioned windows, so different from the arrow-slot apertures of previous years. Before the Battle of Bosworth Sir Rhys, an opportunist, promised Richard III that no man would set foot in west Wales to march against the king 'except over my bellie'. Not willing, or wishing, to oppose Henry Tudor when he landed near Milford Haven, the Welsh nobleman kept his promise by laying down so that the future king could step over his body. After entertaining Henry at Carew he marched with him to

Bosworth, playing a large part in helping his fellow-countryman win the English throne. Rhys was regarded as a 'king-maker' and for his help received rich rewards. Not many years afterwards he organised the finest tournament ever to be seen in Wales. Tents and pavilions were set up in front of the castle, and two hundred retainers waited on the many knights and gentlemen who came to joust and participate in martial sports. At the end of the day Sir Rhys entertained his guests to a banquet in the Great Hall of Carew Castle.

From Carew and from Kilgetty, roads run northwards to join the A40 trunk road. The road from Kilgetty (A478) passes through Narberth, once a fair-sized town but now a village overshadowed by another Norman castle. When Pwyll, Prince of Dyfed, lived here it was known as Arbeth which, according to the *Mabinogion*, was the scene of Pwyll's dealings with Annwvyn (Satan) and

Carew Castle was built about 1270 to replace a 'holding' Norman motte-and-bailey, and must be one of the most elegant and attractive castles in South Wales. Its style represents two periods of architectural history, that of the militant era of the thirteenth century and the fortified manor houses of the fifteenth century. One of the castle owners was Sir John Perrot, reputedly the illegitimate son of King Henry VIII (*Wales Tourist Board*)

of his love for the beautiful Princess Rhiannon. From the main road, between Narberth and Haverfordwest, lanes run northwards through wooded valleys to two other castles at Llawhaden and Wiston, two fortresses in a line dividing the southern, English, part of the county from the Welsh in the north.

The main A40 road ends at Haverfordwest, a place with steep and narrow streets dating from medieval times, peaceful now in comparison with the days when the residents first caught sight of the dreaded Danish longships being rowed up the Cleddau river. In AD 897 the bearded Nordic warriors, armed with huge two-edged swords and battle-axes, terrorised the villagers when they landed here to set up a settlement which they named Hafa's Ford. From then on there was little peace, and about two hundred years later the Normans started to build a castle on a rock high above the river. The Flemings, homeless after their land was flooded, were employed by the Normans to complete the castle, King Henry I saying of them, 'they were a defence against the hostile Welsh'.

The Welsh never ceased attacking the town, but failed to take the castle. Three of their leaders made determined attacks; Gruffydd ap Rhys, then Llywelyn the Great, and in 1405 Glyndwr tried his hand. Conflict continued up to the Civil War when Cromwell, after several attempts, took the castle. Before that event the disturbed people of Haverfordwest suffered an even greater calamity when bubonic plague decimated the population during the months following August 1651. It spread through almost every home and the dead were buried in a communal grave.

Kings and other famous personalities found pleasure in the town, some leaving evident reminders of their visit. It is said that King Henry VIII fathered an illegitimate son, and that Charles II, when he was Prince of Wales, had a son by Lucy Walters after visiting the town in 1648. Poor Lucy's son became the Duke of Monmouth, but such recognition by his father did him little good—he was executed for treason in 1685; thirty years earlier his mother had died penniless in Paris.

Part of the castle is now used as a museum, but the ruins of a keep, drum tower and a curtain wall serve to remind the visitor of its past. Here and there are still traces of the old town walls, and one shop in the main street has the remains of an ancient window and carvings executed in the early sixteenth century.

Seven miles to the south from Haverfordwest along the A4076 is Milford Haven, situated on the north side of a fiord which extends inland for at least twenty miles up to the mouths of the two rivers West and East Cleddau. Hubba, a Viking chief, brought his ships to shelter in the Haven, building settlements along the banks to ensure that hostile tribes would find it difficult to reach and destroy his ships. In later years it was a port of embarkation, for two English kings, Henry II and John, sailed from the Haven to continue the war in Ireland started by Strongbow of Pembroke Castle. Probably to check on the progress of ships being built here during the Napoleonic Wars Lord Nelson made many visits, staying with Sir William and Lady Emma Hamilton at Amroth Castle. The famous admiral considered Milford as 'one of the finest harbours I had ever seen'.

The land-locked stretch of water played a great part in the two world wars. In World War II German planes and U-boats tried to render it useless with mines, and its waterside oil-storage tanks and other installations were continually attacked by Nazi bombers. Now that man has found a new way of obtaining oil from the bed of the ocean the oil refineries are of even greater importance. A short distance eastwards, where the Haven is narrower, is Neyland. There was once a ferry crossing here to Pembroke but this has now been replaced with a fine bridge. The famous engineer Isambard Kingdom Brunel chose Neyland as the starting point for the South Wales to Manchester railway. His *Great Eastern*, the largest ship in the world at its launching in 1858, was berthed here.

Overlooking the western end of the Haven is Dale, a pleasant holiday place situated at the end of the B4327 road from Haverfordwest. It has the reputation of being the sunniest place in Wales. Children now play and build castles on the sands where Henry Tudor landed in 1485 to start his long march to fight for the English crown at Bosworth. It must have also been here that Sir Rhys ap Thomas prostrated himself to allow the future king to step over his 'bellie'. Dale has a long history, but its most prosperous time must have been when it was considered a suitable place for smuggling. If, as is claimed, the village had eighteen inns there would have been good profits for both innkeepers and smugglers. A short way south is St Ann's Head where a lighthouse warns the mariner of dangerous rocks, and the entrance to the Haven.

This south-west tip of the county between the entry into Milford Haven and the southern end of St Bride's Bay is unspoiled. One of the most attractive places is Marloes, a small fishing village, where the lovely sandy bay is seldom crowded as access to the beach is limited. Leech gathering for Harley Street physicians was once a lucrative business here. Some of the leeches, so it is claimed, were used by the local people to innoculate themselves against smallpox. Two islands lie off the coast, Skomer and Skokholm, both private property providing a sanctuary for migratory sea-birds. Further out to sea is the most westerly point of land in Wales.

Beyond Marloes the Nab Headland and the cliffs on either side feel the full force of the Atlantic gales. Just below the rocky Nab is St Bride's where a popularly named Irish saint is said to have been born, perhaps giving her name to a Celtic church for there are many small churches in this part of Wales dedicated to St Bridget. At the southern end of St Bride's Bay at the end of the B4341 road from Haverfordwest are the twin villages of Little Haven and Broad Haven, separated by a steep hill which requires careful negotiation. This is an area popular with those who come to sail their boats in the bay. The Pembrokeshire Countryside Unit, to be found in the car park, provides a range of tours and lectures designed to engender a deeper appreciation of the surrounding countryside and coast. From Broad Haven the road northwards hugs the coastline all the way to Newgale, a small village at the end of a long wind-swept shingle beach. As at Amroth, after severe storms and low tides, the stumps of forest trees are sometimes uncovered. The sea is very cold here, but if this can be tolerated it is a good place for surf bathing.

South-east of Newgale off the A487 is Roch Castle, a designated height where beacon fires were to be lighted if an invading fleet was sighted making its way across St Bride's Bay, or to warn people if Napoleon had swept the English fleet from the Straits of Dover. But a castle existed on this site from the thirteenth century—its purpose to protect its owner from a different kind of invader. Adam de Rupe, or de la Roche, believed a prophecy that he would die of a viper's bite so he built a castle on a rock. However, his precautions were of no avail for one of these venomous creatures was brought into the castle in a bundle of faggots and the prophecy was fulfilled.

After Newgale, the coastline of the bay turns westward to St David's. Halfway along this stretch of the coast is Solva, lying well inland at the end of a fiord-like inlet. This inlet, overlooked by ancient earthworks, is at the mouth of the Solfach river. Follow the river up the valley and you will come to the safest harbour and the most attractive fishing village along the entire coastline of Pembrokeshire. In the Solva valley are attractive colourwashed cottages, corn mills and factories which still make Welsh tweeds and flannel. One mill also specialises in the making of carpets. The first Small Rocks lighthouse was assembled at Solva in 1773. Solva was once a busy trading port, and in 1848 you could sail across the Atlantic to New York for only three pounds, but one had to find five shillings for the booking fee. If you enjoy walking, the road up the river valley with its flower-lined banks is delightful, as is the scenic walk along the edge of the cliffs to St David's which is only three miles away.

There is nowhere in Britain which has finer coastal scenery. Your first walk along these rugged cliffs will be unforgettable, with the cloud-filtered sun colouring the cliffs and casting searchlight rays to form pools of light on misty off-shore islands. Below the edge of the cliffs the sea-birds fly and glide, their shrill cries mingling with the sounds of rolling surf and of huge waves breaking against the rocks below. In sheltered inlets, you might see grey seals basking in the sun.

7

St David's, Fishguard and Cardigan

St David's has been a place of pilgrimage for centuries, and was a centre of Christianity before Canterbury. Anyone making one visit here was considered just as good a Christian as others who had made two journeys to Rome, and to travel here was just as difficult and hazardous. There are two other distinctions: the first, that it is the 'smallest city in Britain'; the second, that the saint, whose bones are interred in the cathedral, was born and bred in his native country. His parents were a prince of Ceredigion (Cardigan) and a noble Celtic lady whose name was used in the dedication of a small chapel and a well. The chapel of St Non has all but disappeared, but the well, still considered holy, was rededicated to the Lady Non in 1951. A few stones marking the site of her chapel can be found in a field south of St David's on the edge of a cliff above a bay which bears her name.

The early Celtic saints set out on long missionary journeys, setting up their simple altars and enclosures, or *llans*, in wild and lonely places. St David occupied a crude hermitage in the Black Mountains valley of Ewyas until he left it to establish a bishopric amidst the pagan remains left by the Romans at Caerleon-on-Usk. Finding the latter a busy and noisy place he moved to Menevia, now called St David's in his honour. The first church would have been very simple, and after Viking raids it was rebuilt many times until the present cathedral was started in about 1180 by Bishop Peter de Leia. About eighty years later Bishop Gower improved it with additions in the new Decorative style of architecture. At the same time he also started to build a splendid episcopal palace around a huge quadrangle.

It is fitting that St David is buried near the spot where he was born, and that he lies in the company of fellow-saints and illustrious people. Saint Caradoc, who died in 1124, has his shrine in the north wall of the transept, and the bones of his friend, St Justinian, lie with those of St David behind the high altar. In front

St David's Cathedral. Known as 'the smallest city in Britain', St David's was a place of pilgrimage for Christians before Canterbury. The bones of St David, who was born nearby, are interred here, and in front of the high altar lies Edmund

of the altar is the tomb of Edmund Tudor whose grandson became a king of England, and at the end of the nave is the tomb of Bishop Gower who did so much to enrich the fabric of this lovely church.

From the west entrance a long flight of stone steps leads up to the village which claims the right to be called a city—a small place, important because of its proximity to the low hollow where a small Celtic *llan* developed to become one of the most beautiful and holy churches in the land. From the centre of St David's roads lead in all directions to many beautiful bays; one is Caerfai where St David often came to bathe. Perhaps Whitesand Bay, or Porth-mawr, is the one most favoured by today's visitors, its sands shielded from the northern winds by St David's Head. At the southern end of the bay is St John's Head overlooking Ramsey Sound and Island, where St Justinian built his Celtic cell. Justinian, a stern disciplinarian, offended some of his followers who subsequently murdered him. According to legend the saint, who had been beheaded, carried his head across the Sound to the mainland, laying it down at Porthstinian where a small chapel was built.

There are two roads from St David's to Fishguard, the most interesting one running reasonably close to the coast. In this, the most exposed part of the county, the roads run for most of the time at a lower level than the adjacent fields. What few trees that grow here are stunted, wind-capped and bent double by the force of south-westerly gales. Lanes run off from the left side of the coastal road to many interesting bays and the ruins of old quays and small hamlets. One such lane runs down to Abereiddy, a pretty bay overlooked by an ancient fort. A turning at Llanrian will take you to Porthgain, where you will find the Sloop Inn which once served ale to fishermen and granite workers. Further along the coastal road is Trefin, or Trevine, a village which once boasted that it was important enough for a bishop to have a palace there, and not far away in a field overlooking the sea is the magnificent cromlech of Carreg Samson. From the cromlech the ground slopes down to the one-time port and shipyard of Abercastle, a picturesque inlet where coal and limestone from Milford was unloaded, and from where ships took cargoes of corn and butter across the Bristol Channel and up through Cardigan Bay to Liverpool.

The coastal road now climbs out of a valley some 300ft up to Mathry, a pre-medieval village where a church is claimed to stand on the site of a pagan stone circle. St Teilo is remembered here as being responsible for the dedication of the church to seven saints; their exact names are unknown, but an old legend records that they were born on the same day, and when their father, a poor man unable to support such a large family, took them to a nearby stream to drown them, St Teilo offered to pay for their upbringing. It is not certain that they all became saints, or even led blameless lives, but it is said that their stone coffins were still to be seen in the churchyard in 1720.

One can follow the coast again up to Pwllderi, a place which must have the finest-sited youth hostel in Britain; behind it towers Garn Fawr, a stone-built fort nearly 600ft above sea level. It is worth the climb for it presents a fine view. On a clear day the hills of Ireland and North Wales can be seen. From this landmark you can go north to Strumble Head and visit a fine lighthouse or turn east to Llanwnda, the place from where Giraldus set out to plead with the Pope for his recognition of St David's as a bishopric. Fishguard Bay and the town are just a few miles away.

The last invasion of the mainland of Britain took place near Fishguard in 1797. The invaders were French, a force of about fourteen hundred led by an Irish-American soldier of fortune named Tate. More than half of them were convicts with little idea of discipline. After climbing the cliffs near Carreg Gwasted the rabble ran wild, terrorising the local peasants and searching for loot, plundering every small cottage or farm they could find. As the result of a wreck along the coast only a few days before, there were not many dwellings which did not have a keg of spirits or wine. The soldiers became so intoxicated that their officers were unable to control them. Troops, and the local people who had armed themselves with all kinds of improvised weapons, mustered to repel the Frenchmen. Tate, unable to control his insubordinate and drunken mob, and mistaking a large number of Welshwomen clad in red cloaks and tall black hats for trained reinforcements, surrendered. One of the Welshwomen, Jemima Nicholas, preferred to take an active part, so after arming herself with a pitchfork she rounded up twelve of the Frenchmen and marched them off to the local jail. A memorial tablet in the church records her deed. A tablet on the external wall of the Royal Oak Inn informs visitors of the attempted invasion, and that a room inside was used for signing the treaty of surrender.

The harbour at Fishguard is deep enough to float the largest ships, and a frequent train service runs along the quay taking passengers to the start of a sea journey across the Irish Sea to Rosslare. From the centre of the town a road winds its way downhill to a smaller harbour at Lower Fishguard. It resembles a small French fishing village spread along the banks of a creek, but nowadays it is a safe haven for the sailing boats owned by members of the club at the end of the quay. It is not a place for the casual visitor, but more for the people who come for week-ends and longer periods in the cottages they own on the hillside above the quay. When the film of *Under Milk Wood* was made Fishguard changed its name to Llaregyb, and when *Moby Dick* was screened an inflated bogus whale was floated from the harbour into the bay.

From Lower Fishguard a lane winds through the Gwaun Valley across the southern slopes of the Preseli Mountains. At the western end of the valley stands Glynamel, a fine period house built by Richard Fenton whose book on Pembrokeshire is recognised as the standard work. A short distance west of Glynamel the valley narrows to a tree-shaded *cwm*, its close contours dictating the course of the rippling Gwaun on its way past charming villages and ancient churches. Time has stood still here as yesterday's ways and traditions are still observed. On the hills above are the remains of many megalithic memorials, alignments and prehistoric tracks.

There is an ancient road along the ridges of the hills, used from Neolithic to Roman times; on top of one hill the Roman Emperor Magnus Maximus pitched his tent, and this site on the summit of Y Frenni Fawr became known as 'the Seat of Maximus'. Earlier, almost two thousand years before the birth of Christ, the ancients dragged and floated huge stones to Salisbury Plain to form an inner circle at Stonehenge. However, a legend disputes this, insisting that the wizard Merlin, scorning such crude and slow means of transportation, caused the stones to dance overland to Salisbury Plain. If this is true the old magician must have lived many years before the days of Arthurian chivalry. The hilltops of Preseli are strewn with the remains of prehistoric settlements, stones of sepulture and circles of pagan worship. A lane will take you to Pentre Ifan, one of the finest and largest cromlechs in Britain. It is at least 16ft long with a massive capstone still supported by three tall upright stones. The peaks and ridges are crowned with other giant stones and relics of ancient man.

Soon after leaving Fishguard eastwards the A487 road reaches Dinas where a headland overlooks Fishguard Bay and Newport Bay with their sandy beaches and old inns. The little town of Newport is at the foot of a hill which still has the ditches and ramparts of an Early Iron Age fort enclosing traces of habitations of the same period. Just north of Newport, on the B4582, is Nevern, a small village connected with Arthurian legends, and with a church said to date back to the sixth century and built by St Brynach. Close to the church is St Brynach's cross, one of the finest pre-Norman monumental crosses in Wales bearing inscriptions in Latin and fifth-century Ogham script. Tegid, a Welsh poet and a man of learning, rests in the churchyard. His tombstone records that he was vicar here for about ten years. The scholarly Tegid assisted Lady Charlotte Guest in translating the stories of the *Mabinogion* from ancient Welsh to English. Near the church are the ruins of a castle which, as it was destroyed after the Normans reached west Wales, is possibly older than any other stone castle in this part of Wales. There exists a strange story that the churchyard yew trees will weep blood until the castle is again occupied by its original Welsh owner; perhaps this is why the stone-flagged path beneath the yews is so often sticky from the red sap which drips from the ancient trees.

North-eastwards from Nevern, at the mouth of the Teifi river, is St Dogmaels—a small fishing village where Sealyham Hall is named as the place where the first Corgi and Sealyham terriers were bred. There are some remains of a twelfth-century abbey in the grounds of the vicarage and nearby is the nineteenth-century Early English-style parish church with a 7ft stone pillar probably dating from the sixth century and also a ninth- or tenth-century pillar carved with a cross.

A fine bridge crosses the Teifi river to the town of Cardigan. It was here, in 1135, that the Welsh fought and defeated the Normans in a battle so fierce that the river ran red with the blood of three thousand Norman soldiers, their bodies providing a human causeway for the victors to cross the river to a town and castle which was rarely out of Welsh hands.

Cardigan (Aberteifi), situated on the north side of the estuary, was once a busy seaport but the Teifi silted up and the trade was lost. It is now a bustling market town. The Teifi Valley, one of the loveliest in Wales, ends at Cardigan, a small town with twisting narrow streets and a Norman castle attracting many visitors. It was from this Norman fortress, or so the story goes, that Owain ap Cadwgan rode off to abduct the Lady Nêst, wife of Gerald de Windsor who was the custodian of Pembroke Castle. Gerald owned so many castles that history has never made up its mind as to which one Owain visited when he rode off to persuade the not unwilling Nêst to live with him in a castle near Llangollen in North Wales. Some historians say that Owain, who must have been the Errol Flynn of his time, took her from Pembroke Castle, others claim that it was from Carew or Cilgerran. Whichever castle it was is not important for the essential details of the abduction are more or less the same. If it was from Cilgerran there is an amusing story of how the bold Owain caused great confusion by setting the castle on fire, so that the unhappy Gerald had to escape from the flames by lowering himself through a garderobe. King Henry I, who had once installed the fickle Nêst as his mistress, banished Owain and took from his father, Prince Cadwgan, land and other possessions. The king replaced the hapless Gerald de Windsor as the custodian of his Welsh castles with Gilbert de Clare. Nêst had many affairs, and her numerous descendants, Welsh and Norman-Welsh, figure largely in Welsh history.

The A487 trunk road out of Cardigan will take the tourist to many interesting coastal and inland places. On the coast is Mwnt, a place known by those who trod the pilgrims' route between St David's and Bardsey Isle at the northern end of Cardigan Bay. When the Flemish landed on the coast in 1155 they were resisted by the Welsh. Very few escaped and for many years afterwards the anniversary of this bloody encounter was celebrated on the first Sunday of January. This celebration was known as 'The Bloody Sunday of Mwnt'. Further along the coast are the popular sandy beaches of Tresaith and Llangranog. The famous English composer Sir Edward Elgar loved this spot and he often walked along the cliff-top paths between Tresaith and Llangranog. One day he heard a group of local choristers practising and harmonising a song on the beach below the cliff. At the time the composer was working on his 'Introduction and Allegro' and although the tune was muted and indistinct enough was heard to help him in his composition. He wrote: 'thinking out my theme, there came up to me the sound of singing. The songs were too far away to reach me distinctly, but fitting the need of the moment I made the little tune which appears in the "Introduction".'

Roads run in almost all directions from Cardigan; the A484 to the south-east follows the Teifi river and soon reaches Cilgerran, a small town with the picturesque ruins of a mighty thirteenth-century castle perched on a rock high above the river. Two famous landscape artists have immortalised the scene, for Cilgerran Castle has been painted by both Joseph Turner and Richard Wilson. When the Normans scaled the rock they faced a ditch and palisade defence, but when the Welsh attacked it in 1165 it had been made more formidable. Judging by the number of times it changed hands it was equally important to both Welsh and Norman.

The road now follows every twist and turn of the Teifi before crossing it at Cenarth, a small riverside hamlet where you can see boats which were used in prehistoric times. These primitive boats—coracles, wicker-framed and skin-covered—were seen and written about in Roman times, and in later years Celtic saints are said to have used them to cross the sea from Ireland. The English are said to have used them to cross French rivers . . . 'boats made very artfully of boiled leather'. It is doubtful if the English could manage them; they were surely manned by Welshmen, who also took with them their dreaded longbows. Cenarth is a delightful place, and from the old four-arched bridge you can see the Teifi foaming and thundering its way through a rocky gorge and over Cenarth Falls. Coracle racing takes place in the Teifi gorge during the summer. Coracles are also used to take fish from the pool below the bridge, and the local farmers drive their sheep into the shallows before they are sheared. In the twelfth century the beaver was found here and, according to Giraldus Cambrensis, this was its last stronghold in England and Wales.

The next river crossing and Norman castle is eastward at Newcastle Emlyn where another road branches off to follow the Teifi to Henllan Bridge. Here the river is joined by other streams, all combining to make an impressive cascade which rushes through a gorge. The fortress at Newcastle Emlyn is more Welsh than

Norman, and if the story is true that Vortigen sheltered there after he was defeated by the Saxons it must be very old. There was enough of the castle left standing after a battering by Glyndwr for Sir Rhys ap Thomas, who helped Henry Tudor pluck the crown of England from a thorn bush at Bosworth, to rebuild it as a riverside home. The town has a busy market, but perhaps it is best known as a centre for fishermen who come to try their luck in fishing the Teifi for salmon, sewin and trout. Allen Raine (Mrs A. Puddicombe), the famous novelist, was born here in 1836. Across the river lies Adpar where the first Welsh printing press was built in 1718 by Isaac Carter. The first Welsh-printed book appeared in 1719, a stone in a house near the bridge commemorating the fact.

Lampeter is about eighteen to twenty miles away eastwards, and a mound in the grounds of a school marks the site of our last Teifiside castle. The superstructure, probably built of wood, was easily taken, destroyed and rebuilt many times. It is said that the town was named Pont-stephan after King Stephen built a bridge over the river. The town is a busy and important tourist centre where many roads converge.

It is said that the 'female of the species is more deadly than the male'. A report (which appeared in the *North Wales Chronicle*) of an event which took place in the town in 1810 confirms this when it stated that 'Two female paupers after a disagreement decided to try skill and strength with cudgels. After fighting for one hour the younger woman, eighty-six, seemed as if she would defeat and kill the elder woman, so the contest was stopped.'

Today the town of Lampeter is famous for more peaceful pursuits, for about twelve years after this female contest the foundations of a theological college were laid, and it was soon allowed to grant the degree of Bachelor of Divinity. Lampeter College is known throughout Britain, and Sir Walter Scott sent his son to the town to study at the local grammar school.

8

Over the Cambrian Mountains and Along the Wye

At almost the highest point alongside the B4519 Eppynt mountain road stand the ruins of the Drovers' Arms, an inn which must have been a welcome sight to the weary cattlemen after their long slog up the steep mountain from Garth. Opposite the ruined inn a concrete spur, built by the military who have shooting ranges here, joins up with the mountain road from Upper Chapel to Builth Wells. After refreshing themselves at the inn the cattlemen drove their herds down the eastern slope of the Eppynt to a ford across the river Wye at Erwood. Had the present river bridge existed then the crossing would have been much easier for all. When the river was flooded men and cattle, bunched closely in large box-like containers, had to be winched across the river. Sometimes the swift current overturned the improvised craft so that man and beast had to swim to the opposite bank. What an epic scene it must have been—exciting enough to provide a thrilling incident in the filming of a Welsh Western.

After fording the Wye the cattle were driven over the hills to Painscastle, and then over the next river crossing at Rhydspence on the Hereford border. The fourteenth-century inn here was a favourite station for the Welsh drovers and they found the local cider particularly good. To avoid the toll-gates the cattle were driven along devious routes. Their destination was Smithfield in London, and for such a long journey they were fitted with steel shoes. In 1820 it was recorded that Welsh cattle on sale in Brighton had come this way. Not all the herds arrived safely, for if there were no painted Indians there were certainly rustlers, and the land was as wild as any to be found in Western America.

A short way from the old Drovers' Arms the mountain road suddenly changes direction to run along the edge of a precipice above a shadowed valley called Cwm Craig Du, then crosses the

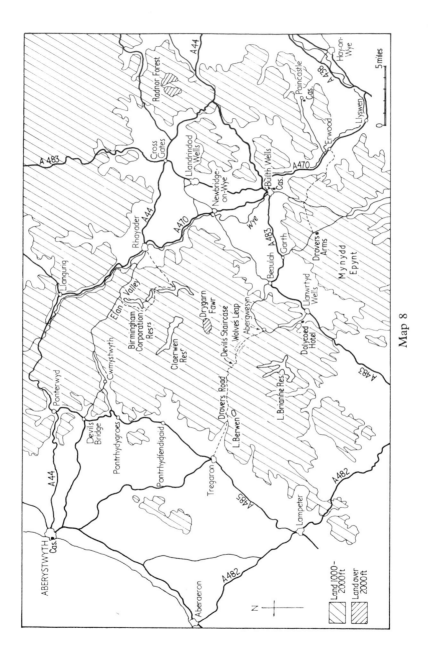

Map 8

Irfon river to join up with the main highway from Builth Wells.

A few miles west is Llanwrtyd Wells, a small town from where one of the most exciting and wildest mountain roads in Wales may be traced—the old drovers' road across the Cambrian Mountains to Tregaron. If, years ago, you had come to Llanwrtyd Wells to taste the spa waters, the chalybeate spring would have been found just outside the town at the Dolycoed Hotel. In the grounds was 'ffynon drellwyd' (the stinking spring) where the Reverend Theophilus Evans came in 1732 to drink the waters. The spring was considered poisonous, but the Reverend Evans, who suffered from scurvy, was desperate to find a cure. He did not have the courage to drink the obnoxious sulphurous liquid, but just as he was about to walk away he saw a frog emerge from the spring, leaping about with unusual vigour. It was an impressive performance and convinced the reverend gentleman that here was the cure for his ailment, so he took a great gulp of the nauseous water and in no time he was cured.

At Llanwrtyd Wells, the river Irfon bends sharply, and up the valley is the old village where there is a church, its site reputed to have been selected by St David. It has few windows and a bell-cote instead of a tower. The hymn writer William Williams Pantycelin was curate here and his portrait hangs on the west wall. The famous preacher Kilsby Jones is buried in the churchyard. He edited a Welsh version of the *Pilgrim's Progress* and translated *Brown's Dictionary of the Bible* into Welsh.

The hamlet of Abergwesyn is some five miles northwards, and the road follows every twist and turn of the Irfon river through a narrow valley of exquisite beauty. The hills on both sides are wooded and wild, their watershed ensuring that the Irfon is always full and its miniature waterfalls always spectacular. Abergwesyn, at the eastern end of the drovers' mountain road from Tregaron, was a convenient place for watering the herds of black cattle before they were driven through Llanwrtyd Wells and over the Eppynt mountain.

At the foot of the notorious Hard Knot Pass in the Lake District a large notice warns that the ascent is steep and difficult. A similar sign points out that the mountain road to Tregaron has 'infrequent passing places' and is very steep and narrow. It soon reaches a narrow ledge cut in the side of the mountain, following the sunlit dancing Irfon winding its way through the valley gorge below.

The road now runs over the out-thrust bases of the hills, and the bends and steep gradients often make it impossible to see what hazards lie ahead. It seems that the road ends at the base of a high mountain, but there is a way over and black V symbols on the map give a warning that the route ahead is very steep and zig-zag. This is 'the Devil's Staircase', and the gorge you have just driven through is known as 'the Wolf's Leap'. It is prudent to select the lowest gear to ensure safe arrival at the high, empty mountain moors. When the writer Bradley came this way about seventy years ago, he wrote:

> Shoulder behind shoulder the northern hills of the valley rear savage heads of rock and the heights of the precipitous cliffs above the scanty turf. Road and river, a ribbon of yellow and a twisting thread of silver wander side by side into a land of mystery.

The first part of the old drovers' road from Abergwesyn to Tregaron runs through the Irfon Valley. The way out of this wild canyon is by way of the formidable track known as 'The Devil's Staircase'. The photograph shows the valley route from the top of the staircase

From the top of 'the Devil's Staircase' the panoramic views are magnificent, but the backward view is the most impressive. On one side of the gorge the narrow track carves its way back to Abergwesyn through the foothills, the Irfon echoing every curve of the track. Like Lakeland screes the mountains rise sheer from the river bank, high and wild, terminating in jagged crags; a wild and savage scene! Here is the haunt of the Red Kite, a rare bird not often seen in other parts of Wales, easily recognised by its forked tail and reddish-brown plumage.

In a few miles, after crossing a stream, the road elbows northwards along a gradient almost as fierce as 'the Devil's Staircase' then descends to a bridge over the Camdwr—a stream of singing water. This lonely way of the drovers crosses many brooks and streams, but this one of the singing water is easily located for it is near its own signpost—a Post Office telephone box. From here a track runs across the moors alongside the Camdwr stream into the magical valleys and hills of Brianne, passing what must be the loneliest chapel in Wales. Years ago the mountain folk rode from their farms to worship at this little chapel, and during the week their children came there to school. Perhaps their tutor may also have been the minister who conducted the Sunday services, and lived in the small house at the end of the chapel. Sanitary arrangements, if primitive, were adequate, for at the end of the building once existed a twin-seater toilet.

Passing the phone box, the drovers' road ascends Esgair Cerig and winds westward past Llyn Berwen, a lonely tarn amid a forestry plantation, winding down the Brenig Valley to make an inconspicuous entry into the Market Square at Tregaron. This town square was once the assembly point of many a cattle drive across the mountains of Mid-Wales to England. The route was rough and stoney, so the drovers saw to it that their herds of black cattle were well prepared for the long journey. The beasts were taken to a field behind the Talbot Hotel where their hooves were fitted with metal plates. Mountain ponies, sheep, pigs and even geese were driven over the mountains; the pigs were shod with woollen socks which had leather soles, and the feet of the geese were prepared by driving them through a mixture of tar and sand. When George Borrow visited the town he was told by an old drover that Tregaron was 'not as big as London, but a very good place'.

Tregaron takes its name from a shepherd boy, Caron, who became king of Ceredigion and was buried here early in the third century. In the town square there is a statue of Henry Richard (1812–88). A Congregational minister, he became MP for Merthyr from 1868 until his death. The church, in its circular churchyard, has an unusual wrought-iron rood screen and a modern stained-glass window featuring the Adoration of the Magi.

For a complete change of scenery, the west coast facing Cardigan Bay is not far away. Aberaeron can be approached through the Vale of Ayron. It is an old-fashioned place, mostly Regency style, with its harbour and fishing boats. It is a popular sailing centre and has a safe beach of gravel and stone. New Quay, a few miles south, is more interesting. It is one of the oldest ports in this area. The harbour, encircled by a headland, provides a sheltered anchorage for yachts. Henry Tudor, on his way to Bosworth, rested near here at the home of Dafydd ap Ieun. Within a year after his visit a child was born to Ieun's daughter, and was called Harry or Parry. For years afterwards anyone named Parry in this part of west Wales claimed a relationship with the first Welsh King of England.

New Quay Head rises to 300ft to the west of the town. Its rocky cliffs contain caves, amongst which is Ogof Ddauben—the 'two-headed cave'. West of the Head is Bird's Rock, a sanctuary for many sea-birds. Across New Quay Bay is Llanina where there is a tiny church on the cliff top.

Because of its geographical situation on the western flank of the Cambrian Mountains Tregaron is a good centre for the tourist. Five roads, counting the old drovers' way, leave the town square, one southwards through the foothills of the mountains, two others westward to the coast; the fifth road follows the course of the Corsgoch Glan Teifi into Mid-Wales. Just before the latter road, the B4343, reaches the small village of Pontrhydfendigaid a narrow lane on the right goes to the abbey of Strata Florida. Here, at one time, was the cultural centre of Wales, and the depository of Welsh National Records. It was also important enough to be the burial place of several Welsh princes; Dafydd ap Gwilym, the great fourteenth-century poet, is also reputedly buried here. In 1284, the abbey was destroyed by King Edward I in revenge for local participation in a rebellion led by Prince Madoc. In later years

King Henry IV and his son Prince Hal of Monmouth used the ruined abbey as headquarters when pursuing the elusive Glyndwr, and when attacking Aberystwyth in 1408. As well as burning down the abbey he set about the destruction of the thickly wooded hillsides which served as cover for the rebels.

At Pontrhydfendigaid, which means Bridge of the Blessed Ford, the Teifi river turns south to flow through the desolate bog of Tregaron, the most miserable mist-covered peat-bog outside Ireland. The next village northwards on the B4343 with a descriptive name is Pontrhydygroes, 'the Bridge near the Ford of the Cross'. This is a favourite haunt of fishermen, for the Ystwyth river flows through a wooded dell just below the village. After several twists and turns the road soon reaches Devil's Bridge where the Mynach and Rheidol streams combine to produce some of the most famous waterfalls in Wales. A deep chasm in the rock forms a 200ft tunnel through which the Mynach plunges in a spectacular cascade. There are three bridges across the Mynach, some sources stating that the lower one was built by the monks of Strata Florida Abbey, but as this spot is marked on the map as Devil's Bridge it is generally accepted that Pont-y-gwr-drwg, 'the Bridge of the Devil', was erected by Satan. A second bridge—a single 20yd span stone segmental arch—was set up above the first in 1753, and the third, of steel construction, was built in 1901. Some two miles south-east on the B4574 road is a memorial arch spanning the road in honour of George III's Jubilee.

This whole area is one of strange stories, ancient mounds, stones of early paganism and a wondrous relic of Christian faith. Near Ponterwyd is an ancient church which stands on a site where the Druids gathered to practise the nauseous ceremonies and rituals of pagan worship. Today the place is known as Parson's Bridge as it was here that the travelling cleric tied up his pony before entering the church. In a secluded valley between the Ystwyth and Rheidol rivers, said to have echoed with the song of nightingales, is the old mansion of Nanteos. Years ago the mansion contained one of the most priceless relics in the world—the remains of a cup claimed to be a portion of the vessel used by Christ at the Last Supper. Throughout the centuries many have searched for the Holy Grail, but it was never thought that it could be found in a valley amid the hills of Mid-Wales. Why was the holy cup brought to Britain; why to Nanteos—and who brought it there? If it was originally brought to Glastonbury by Joseph of Arimathea, when the monasteries were pillaged by King Henry VIII it was reasonable that a safe hiding place should be sought for the chalice amid the Welsh mountains.

Wagner, the composer of the opera *Parsifal*, once stayed here, so the ancient relic may have been his source of inspiration. There are strange stories that those who touched or kissed the cup were cured of disease. Only about sixteen years ago it was recorded that arthritic sufferers found a cure at this house in the valley of the nightingales. It is understood that the owner has taken the precious cup with him to a new home somewhere in Herefordshire.

North of Ponterwyd is the summit of Plynlimon. This mountain is not as spectacular in height or shape as other Welsh mountains; it lacks the grandeur of Snowdon or Tryfan in the north, or the flowing melodic contours of the Brecon Beacons. Its greatest claim to fame is that from its rounded slopes flow two of Britain's most famous rivers. One, the Severn, already anxious to establish itself as an English river, takes an easterly course towards the English border. The Wye, high spirited and as capricious as any Welsh maid, retains a wayward course from Plynlimon to the Bristol Channel. Perhaps this is why the Romans named it the Vaga. After reaching Llangurig, tumbling boisterously through rocky gorges and over falls, the river starts to show its paces.

Most Welsh villages have tales of ghostly visitations and witchcraft. Llangurig, eastwards from Ponterwyd along the A44, has a tale of an elusive hare which could not be shot, some magical quality protecting it from the bullets of the local people. One day a local farmer was told to put a small silver coin into his cartridge instead of the more usual shot. When his silver bullet struck the hare, it screamed with pain and dashed off on three legs. The farmer saw it enter a farm outbuilding, and looking over the half-door he saw an old woman lying on the floor clutching her leg. She told him that she hadn't seen any hare but that she had just broken her leg!

Llangurig lies in a lovely setting and the area is noted for sheep-rearing. Part of the church here is of twelfth-century origin and part is from the fifteenth century. It was much restored in 1878 by J. Y. W. Lloyd who was a curate here. He left the Anglican Church to become a Roman Catholic but eventually returned to Anglicanism. Sir Gilbert Scott was commissioned to carry out the restoration work at a cost of £11,000. Llangurig was at one time noted for its conjurers—not magicians but men with healing powers who were constantly sought to minister to both sick humans and animals.

The A470 road and the River Wye run close together between Llangurig and Rhayader. At Bwlch-gwyn, the river, now well away from its moorland birthplace, flows through a gorge where the rocky bed causes the swift flow to foam so that its former placid surface is broken into miniature 'white horses'. The Welsh meaning of Rhayader is 'cataract', but when the Wye reaches a well-sited caravan site on the outskirts of this town, it almost returns to its former placidity. From the Square at Rhayader, roads run to all points of the compass, but if the visitor can ride a pony this form of transport is the best way to explore the magnificent vari-hued countryside from the surrounding hills.

Straddling the main highway from north to south, the town itself is a busy place. Rhayader is of cruciform shape, its four main streets being named after the points of the compass. There was once a castle here but the only visible remains are a large mound and a few stones. There are some interesting old inns, in particular the Triangle across the river in the Cwmdeuddwr district. It is a partly weather-boarded building dating from the fourteenth century. Cwmddendwr is actually part of Rhayader but it keeps its own identity and has its own church, in the graveyard of which lie the remains of a soldier who fought in the Peninsular War. At Rhayader the Wye is joined by the Elan river flowing from the western moorlands to help to fill the reservoirs of the Elan Valley. These reservoirs supply the industrial Midlands with water—a supply which is charged at a lesser rate in England than in Wales. An elder of the town was once heard to say that 'Owain would have put a stop to that'—there can be little doubt of the truth of this statement.

Beyond Rhayader the Wye, still fairly placid, flows on southwards close to the A470 through flat water-meadows to carve a course through Bwlch-coch, the 'Red Pass', on its way to Newbridge-on-Wye. Here the New Inn offers an ale of excellent quality. It is evidently a good place for man and beast to quench their thirst, for if you should call there about mid-day you will meet one of the regular customers—a large black Labrador dog which calls there every day for his pint of mild and bitter and a bag of crisps. Perhaps he calls twice a day in hot weather?

A short way north-east of Newbridge-on-Wye is the spa town of Llandrindod Wells, making an interesting diversion from the Wye-side journey. Although the general appearance of the town, with its spacious streets and squares, is that of a 'new town' the site was known in Roman times and on the bank of the Ithon river they built Gaer Ddu, 'the Black Fortress'. Excavations carried out between 1911 and 1912 uncovered 8ft thick stone walls together with many copper and silver coins. After establishing themselves here the Romans soon set about searching for medicinal waters, building baths in the locality. In later years it is claimed that King Charles I came here to taste the waters, and on the main road from Builth Wells once stood a milestone inscribed 'To Ye Wells'. Llandrindod used to be the favourite Welsh spa town, and the water here equals that of Bath in quality; it is certainly less obnoxious to the taste than the sulphurous water of Llanwrtyd Wells.

Southwards from Newbridge-on-Wye along the A470 Builth Wells is the next riverside town—a place with a long history and a vivid memory of fierce battles and sieges when the defenders fought hard to protect the river crossing. The Welsh must have fought well for it was at least thirty years before the Norman Marcher Lord, Bernard de Newmarch, was able to build his motte and bailey near the southern bank of the Wye. Even after he built a stronger fortress it was under constant attack from the hill and mountain tribes between Builth and Brecon. Only a mound remains to mark the site of the Norman castle, but a few miles away a large stone stands near the spot where Llywelyn ap Gruffydd, the last Welsh Prince of Wales, was slain in 1282. After decapitation his head is said to have been washed in the well in the garden of a nearby cottage. The gory trophy was sent to King Edward I at Rhuddlan Castle, then to London where, crowned with ivy, it was fixed on a spear high above the battlements of the Tower of London. This fulfilled the prophecy that the prince would wear his crown in London when English money became circular, a change in the shape of the current coinage which actually happened at that time.

Nowadays the town is more peaceful, and in the early summer preparations are made for the Royal Welsh Agricultural Show where the finest selection of Welsh sheep, cattle and horses can be seen. Situated amid fine grazing land the town is conveniently sited for agricultural trading.

It cannot be denied that 'Taffy was a Welshman', but it should not be accepted that he was 'a thief, who came to my house and stole a leg of beef'. It is certain that many portions of tasty beef and succulent *Welsh* mutton would have been found in many a foreign cooking pot! This was a border county with range warfare and rustling a common crime—not a national one, so the first stanza of an old poem would be nearer the truth when it stated that

> The mountain sheep are sweeter,
> But the valley sheep are fatter;
> We therefore deemed it meeter
> To carry off the latter.
> We made an expedition;
> We met a host and quelled it;
> We forced a strong position,
> And killed the men who held it.

The last stanza of this poem proudly boasts that the warriors, apart from stealing sheep, cut off the head of the Welsh chieftain who owned them. After this the Welsh would have taken their revenge, and seen to it that their stockades and larders were replenished.

Just below Builth, off the B4567 between the Eppynt Mountain and the foothills of Radnor, is Aberedw. Here there is a small cave where Prince Llywelyn is supposed to have spent the night before he met his death in 1282. A more likely story is that the cave served as a simple hermitage for a local saint who, according to form, went out of his way to seek the discomfort of a cold, dark penitential cell.

A few miles further south at Erwood, on the A470 road, the Wye with its rocks and rapids provides good sport for the canoeist. The river obstacles are many and difficult so the run should only be attempted by the experienced who must also be expert swimmers. Henry Mayhew is reputed to have stayed here at the local inn and devised the idea of *Punch* magazine during his sojourn.

Near Llyswen, still further south along the A470, between the road and the river is the large mansion of Llangoed, a substantial home with many rooms and three large galleries built one above the other. It was once owned by the same family who offered hospitality to King Charles I at Gwernyfed near Talgarth. By some dubious means, rumoured to be in payment of a gambling debt, the Wye-side mansion fell into the hands of a Regency rake named Macnamara. He was a wild character who had another home called The Hermitage in a secluded Black Mountain valley. This latter house served as a home for his mistress, and the story is still told of mad Macnamara driving a coach and four over the mountains to visit her. A track from The Hermitage over the mountain is, in places, still visible.

The last riverside town on our route is Hay-on-Wye. It is only just in Wales, so as a border town it must have seen a fair amount of strife and trouble. At one time, as the population of the town was varied, it was divided into Welsh Hay and English Hay to satisfy all. Although officially in Wales the town seems more English than Welsh, but any town in the marches of Wales was vulnerable to the attentions of Owain Glyndwr. Hay is blessed, or cursed, with two castles. Little is left of the first motte and bailey and the other, part fortress, part mansion, has twice been gutted by fire.

If you wish to purchase a book which you have not been able to find anywhere else, it is a fairly safe bet that you will find it in Hay. Booth's Bookshops are becoming internationally known, and visitors from all parts of the world come here in search of an elusive or out of print volume. There are bookshops in every street; even the local cinema has been converted into a large book-store and warehouse where second-hand books are bought and sold. This market town was once the centre for the flannel industry but is now a focus for the farming fraternity, the sales of Clun and Kerry sheep taking place at the Smithfield, or market.

King Henry II visited Hay when he sought the favours of a young maid who lived at Clifford Castle, the furthest western fortress from which the Normans commanded the upper Wye valley. Fair Rosamund, the young maid who became mistress of a king of England, was made famous by bard and poet, much to the displeasure of Eleanor, wife of Henry II. According to a poem by Tennyson, the young lady of Clifford Castle was not always happy with the king's attentions. The poet wrote:

Turn round and look on me,
I am that Rosamund that men call fair,
If what I was I be,
Would I had been some maiden coarse and poor,
O me! that I should ever see the light!
Those dragon eyes of angered Eleanor
Do hurt me day and night.

To visit Clifford today one must cross the border into England, but not *all* of Hereford was always in England so such trespass is excusable. Indeed, this English county with such place-names as Llandibo, Llangarran and Llanrothal suggests an earlier Welsh nationality. Llanrothal has a monument to one named William Gwillym; what could be more Welsh than this? And in 1189 King Richard I offered a Charter '. . . to our citizens of Hereford *in Wales*'.

From the border town of Hay-on-Wye the river pursues a sinuous course through the flat green pastureland of west Hereford, losing its Welshness on its journey through apple

Because of its wayward wandering course the Romans called the Wye the Vaga, but here, where it almost touches the A438 road between Clyro and Rhydspence, it runs in a straight line to the foothills of the Black Mountains. Across the river is the castle of Clifford, the home of beautiful Rosamund who became the mistress of Henry II

orchards and hamlets of picturesque half-timbered inns and cottages—a land where even the white-faced cattle look different, and the former dramatic scenery of Wales is replaced by views which have a rustic pictorial quality. The noise and clash of arms in battle have been left behind, giving the impression that this land was always peaceful.

After flowing through English towns and fields the Wye regains its Welsh identity on the outskirts of Monmouth, then carves a way between the wooded cliffs of the beautiful Wye Valley to Tintern. From its beginnings in the bleak, rounded slopes of Plynlimon the Wye comes to Chepstow where the river crossing is dominated by a Norman castle built on one of the most picturesque sites in Britain. Below Chepstow the Wye flows into the Severn Estuary, joining the waters which also had an insignificant birthplace among the wild and lonely mountains of Mid-Wales.

9

The Lakes of Mid-Wales

Ask the average tourist what picture he has of Wales; his mental image will generally project scenes of high mountains and steep roads running along the edge of deep ravines through windswept passes. After further prompting he will most likely remember that Wales has Druids who still practise bardic rites, and then Owain Glyndwr, Dylan Thomas, and Wynford Vaughan-Thomas, castles and coal pits.

This land of Wales has other splendours, for there are lakes and waterfalls as beautiful as any to be found in the Lakeland of northern Britain. The beautiful Llyn Brianne, among the Cambrian mountains of West Wales, has already been visited, but perhaps the most lovely lakes are situated in the centre of Mid-Wales.

The gateway to this Welsh Lakeland is Rhayader, a small town on the bank of the Wye which gives convenient access to the Elan and Claerwen valleys, and a chain of man-made lakes. These fertile and wooded valleys were flooded to supply water for the industrial towns of the English midlands, and every day some 60 million gallons of water flow through a seventy-mile-long line of pipes to Birmingham. From Rhayader's town square the B4518 road runs south-west to Caban Coch, and after crossing the head of this reservoir it then winds a way through the Claerwen Valley, ending at a car park near the top of the high concrete dam which holds back the waters of the Afon Claerwen Reservoir. This gigantic dam was opened after the Second World War by Queen Elizabeth II. North of the first reservoir, Caban Coch, forming a sparkling chain of sunlit water, are the reservoirs of Garreg Ddu, Pen-y-Garreg and Craig-yr-Allt Goch, the hard rock floor of the Elan valley gorge providing a firm natural foundation for the dams.

When the day came to flood the valleys, cottages and mansions in the water's path were demolished. One of the finest houses was Cwm Elan where the poet Shelley lived after he was sent down

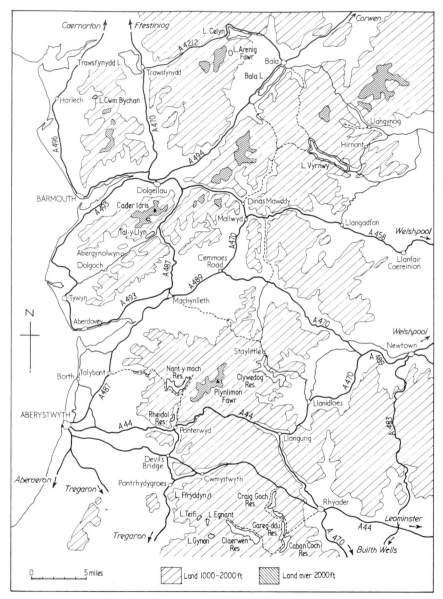

Map 9

from Oxford. This valley hidden in the Welsh mountains was his Shangri La, and after his marriage it was not long before he returned with his bride to the Elan Valley where they made their home at another house named Nantgwyllt. The house now lies beneath the deep waters of Caban Coch, and it became the inspiration for Francis Brett Young to write his well-known novel—*The House under the Water*.

Roads run on both sides of the lake. After running through the soggy moorlands between the mountains and the western shoreline of Craig-yr-Allt Reservoir the road reaches, at Pont ar Elan, a junction above the point where the Elan river flows into the reservoir. In the days of prehistory this must have been an important junction, for the map shows that several 'Ancient Roads' met here. Even on a fairly bright day the way north appears wild and bleak, the changing direction of the mountain road and river being dictated by the foothills of the mountains. Before Cwmstwyth is reached road and river go their separate ways through different valleys. There are the ruins of lead mines in this area which were worked for centuries after the Romans left them. In the fourteenth century they were worked by the monks of Strata Florida Abbey, one of the largest and most productive mines being at Cwmystwyth.

After reaching Devil's Bridge the old miners' road joins the main highway to Aberystwyth at Ponterwyd. Here you can learn how the precious lead was worked during the mining boom of the 1870s. There is an open air museum, and everything possible has been done to inform and interest the tourist. In a floodlit underground cavern are scenes of mining activities, and to make the process of mining even clearer there is an explanatory slide-show. The exhibition is open from Easter to September.

Having visited the beautiful Elan Valley it seems logical to extend this 'water-tour' to see other lakes in this area of Mid-Wales. After driving eastwards on the A44 to Llangurig, take the A470 to Llanidloes, an attractive market town with tree-lined streets, a unique half timbered market house, a parish church of thirteenth-century origins with sixteenth-century additions, and some interesting shop fronts. At Llanidloes, you will have reached the centre of Wales, at the junction of the Severn and Clywedog rivers. There are not very many 'black and white' timbered

Pen-y-garreg Reservoir. Take the old coach road out of Rhayader to Devil's Bridge and in a short time you will be able to drive around the perimeter of nine miles of lakes. All are situated in the beautiful valleys of Elan and Claerwen. Rhayader is a tourist centre, popular with fishermen, ramblers and those who wish to ride among the surrounding hills

buildings in this part of Wales, but the early seventeenth-century Market Hall in the town square is a fine example of this form of architectural design and construction. It has been used as an Assize Court and John Wesley came there to preach. Today it is a museum housing relics of lead mining and other local industries. In 1839 the town and district was a meeting place for the Chartists until the military were called in to arrest them. These early trade unionists, lacking effective weapons, were not able to offer much resistance for, according to a local rhyme,

> The rebels had a bullet mould,
> A pistol rusty, crack'd and old,
> Some bellows, pipes, and lucifers,
> Tweezers, card-plates, and goose-oil cans,
> With dust and other nameless pans,
> Hot water, soapsuds, toasting prongs,
> With cat-calls, horns, and women's tongues.

They hid amid the surrounding hills, but the soldiers captured thirty of them who were sentenced to imprisonment or deportation.

From the Market Hall a road, the B4518, climbs a hillside. In about two miles the car can be parked, and you can then look down over a massive dam and the lake of Clywedog. The Midlands industries, still thirsty for more water, obtain an additional supply from this seven-mile-long reservoir in a valley to the east of Plynlimon Fawr. From the dam, after negotiating two horseshoe bends past an ancient *caer*, the road runs northwards along the lower slopes of Mynydd Groes. All the way there are viewpoints over the man-made lake and the distant hills. After crossing a tributary stream, and driving through pretty woodland you come to the hamlet of Staylittle. If you wish to complete a round tour of the lake a road from this point will bring you back to the dam and the starting point of your lakeside journey.

Staylittle is so named in recognition of two local blacksmiths. They evidently enjoyed and took pride in their work. Unhampered by the modern dictates of time and motion and other restrictive rules, the two smiths shod horses so rapidly that it was necessary for their riders only to 'stay-a-little', so this name was given to their forge. An interesting feature is a Quaker burial ground on the hillside here.

For an exciting drive through more wild Welsh scenery, after leaving Staylittle on the B4518 take a lane on the left signposted Dylife, another place where the earth was torn apart for silver and lead. Just before reaching Dylife the lane bridges the head of a gorge where steep mountains rise almost vertically on both sides. It is so steep that the Afon Twynyn at the bottom of the ravine must always be in flood. Ffrwd Fawr, one of the highest Welsh waterfalls, drops from the upland moors into the river valley. From the high mountain road the view up the gorge is one of breathtaking magnificence.

There are not many people living today in Dylife, for there seems to be no other building here except the Star Inn, unless the ruined surface buildings of disused mineworkings are counted. Stories are told in the inn of the days when the lead mines and the tavern were both busy. Another tale is that of a dreadful murder. About a hundred years ago those travelling along the lonely mountain road at night must surely have shuddered and crossed themselves when they came in sight of a roadside gibbet. Suspended from a projecting beam they would have seen, illuminated by the moonlight, a rusting metal cage, and inside it a decaying, almost skeletal figure wearing an iron headpiece. The story goes that when one of the mineworkers was accused by his wife of being unfaithful, he murdered her and his young daughter and threw their bodies down a disused mine shaft. He made plausible excuses regarding their absence, but when their bodies were eventually discovered he was condemned to hang in chains and, as was the custom, to first forge his own headpiece. When the wooden gallows rotted away and his corpse fell to the ground the metal helmet was buried there. Several years afterwards it was discovered and is now displayed as an interesting relic of the past at the Folk Museum at St Fagan's near Cardiff (see page 56).

Northwards from this haunted spot Nant-y-fyda is reached near the junction of two mountain streams which combine to form the Afon Dulas. At this point the bleak moors and mountains are left behind, and the prospect ahead becomes pastoral. Across the Dovey Valley and estuary can be seen the irregular dim blue outlines of the higher mountains of Wales, from Cader Idris up to

The scenery around the Afon Twynyn Gorge near Dylife is wild, and here the mountain road to Machynlleth bridges the head of a gorge where the mountains rise almost vertically on both sides. On the left of the gorge the Ffrwd Fawr waterfall drops from the upland moors into the ravine

the majestic ranges of Snowdonia. From the moors the road descends, keeping close company with the silvery tumbling Dulas and crossing the stream just before reaching Machynlleth, the gateway to the beautiful Vale of Dovey.

Machynlleth is a tourist centre, and in the summer months the wide streets are thronged with visitors. Centuries ago the small town was important enough for Owain Glyndwr to establish there his Parliament House, making the town his capital. Some sources claim that he ruled from Dolgellau, but an ancient stone building in the centre of Machynlleth is still known as Glyndwr's Parliament House. His seal was adopted by the town as its own official seal. The town may have been important to the Romans, for two miles away at Pennal lead and silver were collected for shipment to Rome.

Glyndwr must have felt safe here in the heart of Wales and among his countrymen, for when David Gam, a favourite squire of Prince Henry of Monmouth, rode from South Wales to assassinate him, he was soon captured and put in prison. The Welsh leader never forgave Gam for his treacherous behaviour, and when he had reason to lead an army to South Wales he made certain that Gam would always remember his visit—he rode into Brecon and set fire to his house. For some reason Glyndwr, completely out of character, could not bring himself to execute his fellow-countryman, and after ten years Gam was allowed to return to South Wales. Soon afterwards he was knighted on the battlefield before dying from wounds received in protecting King Henry V at Agincourt. When he was asked by the king to report on the French numbers, he said, 'There are enough to kill, enough to be taken prisoner and enough to run away.'

Machynlleth is a 'T'-shaped town, the upright of the 'T' being the main street. At the far end of this tree-lined road of shops stands the old Maerdy or Court House, whose timbered front bears the date 1628. Plas Machynlleth, a large seventeenth-century mansion and estate, is the seat of municipal government. The property was presented to the town by Lord Londonderry in 1949. The town's Clock Tower was erected by public subscription in 1873. In the eighteenth and nineteenth centuries there were many printing houses here together with a snuff factory. At one time the town boasted twenty-four inns, two of which remain.

From the town square it is not easy to decide the most interesting route to take, but it seems logical to complete our tour of the Welsh lakes in this area. To do so follow the A487 Aberystwyth road. The first stop along this road must certainly be at Caerhedyn. From here you can walk up the Llyfnant Valley alongside a clear green stream, and there are miniature waterfalls every hundred yards or so. After a few miles through this beautiful valley you will reach Glaspwll where it is joined by another valley going north towards Machynlleth. The toe of Cefn Coch forces the track to turn southwards to Cwmyrhaiadr where another mountain causes the stream to divide. Taking the right fork you will soon reach the 300ft high waterfall of Pistyll-y-Llyn. If you still feel energetic enough to explore more of these delectable river valleys continue south to the twin lakes of Llyn Conach and Llyn Dwin, and on the way you will pass the Angler's Retreat, a small pool at the side of Llyn Plas-y-mynydd.

The next stop along the road to Aberystwyth is at Furnace. It is not hard to understand the reason for its name. In the days of mining for silver and lead there was a small smeltery here, and the Einon river with its picturesque waterfall provided strong waterpower to turn the wheels and cogs of the workings. Remains of the original water-wheel which drove the machinery and operated the blast furnace can no longer be seen; the present wheel is of a later date. From the site of the old workings a steep lane leads to another valley, so lovely that it deserves its name: 'Artists' Valley'. The narrow lane runs along the edge of Cwm Einon gorge, so it is fortunate that there are several passing places. Near a point where an ill-defined track goes to a deserted lead mine there is a picnic spot known as Forester's Lodge, but if you wish to follow a track alongside the Einon stream back to the twin lakes of Llyn Dwin and Llyn Conach it is best to walk.

The next village on the A487 is Taliesin, named after a famous Welsh bard whose grave is sited on a moorland east of the village and clearly marked on the map as Bedd Taliesin. Why such a well-loved bard was buried in this lonely and almost inaccessible spot it is difficult to understand. If you do want to pay your respects to Taliesin the easiest way to reach his grave is to follow the lane which runs in a north-easterly direction from Talybont village, the next village along our route.

Another lake on our tour of the Lakeland of Mid-Wales can be reached from Talybont, where a lane is signposted to Nant-y-moch. After going through a narrow gorge the road, having a fair surface, follows the Ceulan stream, but becomes less defined until it finally meets a track coming from the north and the Vale of Cwm Einon. At this junction the track soon passes an old lead mine and a small tarn, one of a chain which helps to fill the Nant-y-moch reservoir. The track, although stoney, becomes more defined as it follows the edge of the reservoir all the way up to the large concrete dam where the overspill flows into the Afon Rheidol. As you cross the dam you will see directly in front of you the summit of Plynlimon and the source of the River Wye. All the way from Talybont the countryside is impressive for bleak wildness rather than beauty, but it is always interesting. After passing the minor reservoir of Dinas the unfenced road reaches Ponterwyd on the main A44 trunk road to Aberystwyth.

Aberystwyth, fronting Cardigan Bay, is an ideal centre for exploration of the coastal region to north and south. With many Victorian and Georgian buildings the town does not seem to be very old, but as King Edward I built one of his castles here it has a history which goes back many years. The reason for choosing a particular site on which to erect a fortress was often indicated by the remains of a prehistoric camp, and here the Normans followed the example of the early coastal dwellers who engineered their earthworks on a hilltop between the coastal entry of the Rheidol and Ystwyth rivers into Cardigan Bay. So the ancient earthwork on Pen Dinas is as interesting as the ruins of the Edwardian castle which after being battered many times by the Welsh was finally dismantled by Cromwell, but during the Civil War it was used as a Royal Mint.

At Aberystwyth every high point above the town has become important. At the north end of the wide bay a funicular railway will take you up to the top of Constitutional Hill where there are fine views over the town, the coastline and the surrounding country-side. On another hill stand the modern buildings of the University College of Wales, and on the same hill is the National Library of Wales. The library contains the oldest Welsh manu-script in existence, *The Black Book of Carmarthen*. The shelves also support other priceless books and manuscripts, works by Bede and

Geoffrey of Monmouth, a manuscript copy of Chaucer's *Canterbury Tales* and the oldest known copy of the *Mabinogion*, a strange collection of tales passed down through the ages by word of mouth until, in the Middle Ages, they were recorded. The tales of early saints and knights gave inspiration to Malory and Lord Tennyson.

From the centre of the town the Rheidol Valley narrow-gauge railway runs for twelve miles or more through a valley of exquisite beauty. It follows the Afon Rheidol all the way from Aberystwyth to Devil's Bridge, stopping at several halts from which you may alight to explore the riverside heights and waterfalls. The railway, first laid down in 1902, was used to transport lead and other ores from the mines for shipment from Aberystwyth.

It is eighteen miles along the A487 from Aberystwyth back to Machynlleth, the most convenient place from which to journey to other beautiful places in this area of Wales. Follow the Afon Dovey via the B4404 to Cemmaes Road Junction then along the A470 to Mallwyd. From there you can go over Bwlch-y-Oerdrws, 'the Pass of the Cold Door', or venture over the more formidable Bwlch-y-Groes, 'the Pass of the Cross'. Dinas Mawddy, a short distance further north on the A470, is the starting point for both mountain passes, but if you have read about this area it is certain that the latter *bwlch* will be chosen.

At Mallwyd, a brochure in the bar of the Brigand's Inn will persuade the adventurous tourist to climb the Aran mountain road, feeling secure that today he will not be ambushed and robbed by the red-haired bandits of Dinas Mawddy—the local Mafia who met and made their plans in a room at the inn. The road from Dinas Mawddy climbing over the mountains to Bala is the highest and steepest in Wales. The adjoining mountains were once the retreat of the red-haired bandits. During the reign of Queen Mary they terrorised the district, robbing and murdering any traveller reckless enough to take the Bwlch-y-Groes road. They plagued the district for years until, on Christmas Eve, a force of men led by a local baron captured eighty of the brigands. Among those condemned to hang were two youths whose mother pleaded for their lives. When her pleas were refused she cursed the baron, saying that one day her compatriots would wash their hands in his blood. Her prophecy came true for soon afterwards the baron and his son, on their way to a local court, were pulled from their coach and stabbed to death. The spot where this happened is now known as Llidiart-y-Barwn, 'the Baron's Gate'. Many years later George Borrow wrote that he found at Dinas Mawddy 'a collection of filthy huts with fierce red-haired men staggering about, looking like the descendants of the robbers of centuries before'.

There are several legends concerning this mountain pass. One, which explains its name, tells of a traveller who, suddenly aware that he was being followed by an evil-looking man, thankfully saw ahead of him a figure riding a white stallion. When he reached the rider they rode together in silence, the hooves of the white stallion making no sound on the rough mountain road. On looking back the traveller saw the potential highwayman turn and ride away. Turning to thank the kindly horseman he found that rider and mount had vanished. Convinced that some heavenly intervention had saved him the traveller arranged for a cross to be erected by the wayside. Another legend tells of how a local giant named Rhitta, a collector of the beards of the famous people he had slain, fought with King Arthur, attempting to cut off his long golden beard. He was no match for Arthur who, with one quick stroke of his magic sword Excalibur, sliced off the giant's head and tumbled his body into a deep gully. The way down to Tan-y-bwlch is called Rhiw Barfe, 'the Way of the Bearded One'.

The summit of the Bwlch-y-Groes is almost 1,800ft above sea level, and the very steep road up to it runs along a narrow shelf above a deep ravine, so in order to ensure a safe arrival at the top of the pass it is advisable to concentrate on your driving before making an appraisal of the mountain scenery. Daniel Defoe was more impressed with the Welsh mountain scenery than any he had seen during a journey through South America. When he wrote the following lines it is probable that he was looking down from the top of the Bwlch-y-Groes towards Dinas Mawddy:

> They stand together and they are as Mountains piled upon Mountains, Hills upon Hills. Whereas we sometimes see these Mountains rising up at once from the lowest Valleys to the highest Summits, which makes the Height look horrid and frightful, even worse than the Mountains abroad.

He must have been considerably impressed for he also wrote that 'the Devil lives in the Middle of Wales'.

From the car park at the summit there are expansive views of the nearby mountain scenery, and on a clear day the mountains of Snowdonia are visible. Just before reaching the summit a track on the right runs down the mountain to Lake Vyrnwy. This lake was filled by numerous streams from the surrounding hills, and through the pass of Bwlch-y-Groes the Afon Cedig rushes down the Berwyn mountains to add a further liquid contribution. When Liverpool thirsted for this Welsh water, after drowning one village they replaced it with another which was built in the shelter of the dam and named Llanwddyn. A well-surfaced road, part of the B4393, runs round the perimeter of the lake—a distance of ten miles. The lake lies deep in the Hirnant valley, and after driving around the lake a road at its northern end will take you to Bala. The first section of the road goes through tree-shaded *cwms* following a mountain stream as far as Bwlch Rhiw Hirnant, a spectacular pass over 2,000ft above sea level. From here it descends steeply down to the northern end of Llyn Bala.

Most Welsh lakes have legends of fairy maidens, hobgoblins and the sound of bells ringing from submerged towers, so to be in fashion, the lakeside of Bala is haunted by a phantom harpist whose sweet music, capturing the mood and rhythmic movements of the waters of this beautiful lake, can be heard at twilight. Fed by the Afon Dee which flows from the Arenig mountains, Bala claims to be the largest natural freshwater lake in Wales. Bala town is conveniently situated for the tourist wishing to explore North Wales, and a picturesque road winds along the Vale of Edeyrnion through Corwen to the lovely Dee-side town of Llangollen. In the height of summer one has the impression that Bala is a lively friendly place, with a wide main street lined with many comfortable hotels and guest houses. George Borrow, who appreciated good ale, found it very much to his liking at the White Lion Hotel.

Bala was once famous for its knitted stockings—George III insisted on wearing them to aid his rheumatism. That industry has long since died and Bala is probably better known as one of the leading centres of the nonconformist movement in Wales. One of the foremost figures concerned was Thomas Charles whose statue stands in Tegid Street. He set up a chain of Sunday schools, attended by both children and adults. As a result, thousands of Welsh bibles were produced and distributed. Charles was one of the founders of the British and Foreign Bible Society. In turn, his grandson, David Charles, was one of the founders of the Calvinistic Methodist College in the hills above Bala in 1837. Another memorial in Bala is that of Tom Ellis MP, which stands in the main street. Ellis became Liberal Chief Whip but his career was much shortened by his untimely death at the age of forty.

There seems to be no record of Norman occupation of Bala, but in a side street behind the old grammar school there is a small mound which may have once been part of a motte-and bailey fortress. It is known as Tomen-y-Bala, and as it was captured by the Welsh in 1202 it may have then been held by the Normans. There is less doubt of Roman occupation, for near the south end of the lake there are traces of their fort of Gaer Gai. From here you can drive through the Wnion Valley via the A494 to Dolgellau, or back to Machynlleth, the starting point of our journey to the lakes of Vyrnwy and Bala.

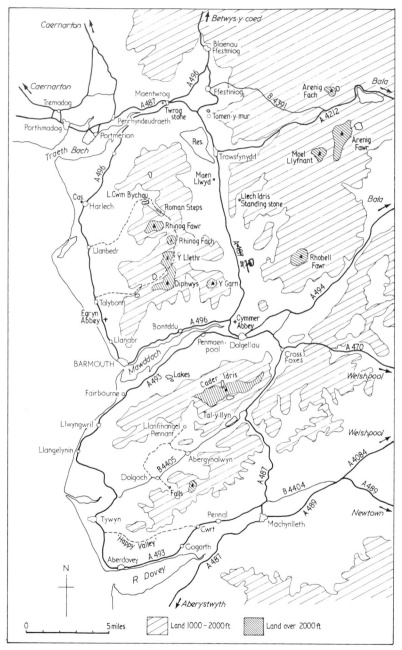

Caernarfon

Betws-y-coed

Blaenau Ffestiniog

Caernarfon

Bala

Tremadog

Maentwrog

Ffestiniog

Arenig Fach

Porthmadog

Portmeirion

Penrhyndeudraeth

A 487

Twrog stone

Tomen-y-mur

B 4391

A 4212

Traeth Bach

A 496

Res.

Trawsfynydd

Moel Llyfnant

Arenig Fawr

Maen Llwyd

Cas.

Harlech

L.Cwm Bychau

Roman Steps

Llech Idris Standing stone

Bala

Rhinog Fawr

Llanbedr

Rhinog Fach

Y Llethr

A 487

Rhobell Fawr

Diphwys

Y Garn

Talybont

A 494

Egryn Abbey

Llanabr

Bontddu

A 496

Cymmer Abbey

BARMOUTH

Mawddach

Penmaenpool

Dolgellau

Cross Foxes

A 470

A 493

Lakes

Cader Idris

Welshpool

Fairbourne

Tal-y-llyn

Llwyngwril

Llanfihangel Pennant

Welshpool

Llangelynin

A 4084

B 4405

Abergynolwyn

A 487

A 489

Dolgoch

B 4404

Newtown

Falls

Pennal

A 489

Tywyn

Cwrt

Machynlleth

Happy Valley

Gogarth

Aberdovey

A 493

A 487

N

R Dovey

Aberystwyth

0   5 miles

Land 1000 – 2000 ft

Land over 2000 ft

Map 10

10

The Estuaries of Mid-Wales

If you decide to take the coastal A487 through this part of Wales, after reaching Aberystwyth the road swings inland and away from the estuary of the Dovey. To reach the far side of this wide stretch of water the nearest crossing is just north of Machynlleth, then after turning west along the A493 you will probably be driving along the same route that the Romans used to reach Pennal where a small rectangular mound marks the site of their fort. They called this fort Cefn Caer, and built it to protect the passage across the Dovey.

About a mile further along the A493 is Cwrt where a track on the right leads off the main Aberdovey road. This track was once the main coach road to Towyn, but today the coastal estuary road is used. Even a cursory glance at the map will convince you that exploration of the old road is irresistible; leave it and climb to the top of Allt-y-Tyddyn-y-Briddell from which are splendid views of the Dovey estuary and the coast as far as Constitutional Hill above Aberystwyth. Further south are the lower mountain peaks of Mid-Wales and, rising above them the smooth whale-back hump of Plynlimon.

A full day is hardly long enough to explore this fascinating upland above the estuary. There is something to interest everyone, artist, poet or historian; in fact all who are thrilled by relics and mysterious legends of the past. A stony walker's track leads to a lake associated with King Arthur. It is called Llyn Barfog, which means 'the Bearded Lake', so it may have something to do with his long golden beard. This is another lonely tarn from which a fairy maid came to marry a mortal—but returned to the bottom of the lake when he failed to comply with the conditions of her acceptance of him in marriage. There are no records of these lakeside betrothals ever reaching the fairy-tale ending of 'living happy ever after'. Legends of the beautiful but over-sensitive lake maidens, not being able to tolerate harsh words or the touch of iron, are common in all parts of Britain. Stories through the ages have endowed metal with magical qualities. Many folk living in South Wales will remember the old game called 'tag' which went as follows. One of the many players pursued his friends, and when he was able to 'tag' or touch him it was then that player's turn to become the pursuer. If the pursued player managed to grasp a section of metal rail or gate he announced that he was 'holding iron', and in this state of sanctuary he could not be 'tagged'. Similar legends from the past are connected with many other childhood games. Did King Arthur come here in search of a romantic lakeside dalliance? Perhaps he did, for a stone marked on the map as Carn March Arthur is supposed to bear the imprint of his horse's hooves.

It is said that Llyn Barfog was once occupied by lake-dwellers, and near the lake are circles of heaped stones which may be the lower stone courses of the round-houses of those primitive times. Finds of stone axe and hammer heads offer proof of prehistoric occupation. At a point where the road emerges into a wide valley it is marked on the maps as 'Happy Valley'. Does this suggest that the people who lived here were happy folk, and a close community content with the beauty and seclusion of their home in the mountains above the Dovey estuary? Soon after passing a tumulus and a disused lead mine the track drops down to join the coastal road again.

From Cwrt the A493 follows the curvaceous coast to Aber-dovey, a picturesque resort sited on a terrace of rock between the hills and the estuary. A narrow tongue of marshland and sand reduces the width of the entry from Cardigan Bay to provide a safe haven for ships seeking shelter from the south-westerly gales. Today, with the road curving around minor bays below rising terraces of houses, one's first impression is of entering a Continental fishing port. Years ago ships from many parts of the world sailed into the small harbour, making it a busy and prosperous port, and during the eighteenth century it was the scene of smuggling activities. Ancient stories claim that here was the site of Cantre'r Gwaelod, a fine proud city until the neglected and crumbling dykes broke to allow the high sea from Cardigan Bay to drown it. An old song, a favourite of Welsh harpists, tells of a city beneath the sea. The title of the song is 'The Bells of Aberdovey', and for many years people have sworn that they can sometimes hear the chiming of bells from the drowned city. The Outward Bound Sea School is located at Aberdovey.

Next along the coastal road is Tywyn or Towyn, a holiday resort with a long stretch of sand which stretches back as far as Aberdovey. There is everything else to attract the seaside visitor, but there is very little to say about these obvious attractions, for it is certain that the tourist will find more interest in the ancient church of St Cadfan of Brittany. Inside the church is the old saint's stone, 7ft high, a relic of the seventh century with an inscription in early Welsh centuries older than any other known writing. When he established his church here in the sixth century, Cadfan, as many of his fellow-saints did, sanctified the waters of a well to perpetuate his memory, and this well was considered one which provided a certain cure for gout and rheumatism. The present Church of St Cadfan is of twelfth-century foundation. During the 1880s the building was extensively restored. It contains two fourteenth-century effigies—one of a priest with his head covered, the other of a knight; also an old bass viol and a carved organ case.

From Tywyn the A493 runs along the coast and round the scenic Mawddach Estuary to Dolgellau, but the inland route via the B4405, about the same distance, is far more interesting. The road and the miniature Talyllyn Railway runs alongside the foothills of Cader Idris towards the lovely lake of Tal-y-llyn. The railway conveys thousands of summer visitors to Dolgoch Halt, from where a short walk ends beneath another beautiful waterfall. In fact there are three falls, and the way to all three through a wooded ravine is well sign-posted. The return walk goes through Coed Dolgoch and the entire circuit can easily be completed in about one and a half hours.

On both sides of the valley the tops of the mountains are often hidden in cloud, and from the close-contoured 2,000ft height of Mynydd Esgair-weddon the Dolgoch stream rushes down a narrow *cwm* to the falls. At Abergynolwyn, below a spur of the mighty Cader Idris, a narrow cleft in the hills between Gamallt Hill and Moel Caer-berllan allows a lane and the Afon Dysynni through to Dyffryn Dysynni, a green valley dominated by the fortress of Castell-y-Bere. Nearby, built on a high ridge below the village of Llanvihangel-y-Pennant the castle stands on one of the most dramatic sites in Wales. The Welsh were quick to learn the art of building castles from the Normans, and they erected this fortress on a precipitous ledge of rock commanding two valleys. After a long siege and a bloody assault King Edward I managed to take the castle. Realising it was a post of great military importance he raised the height of the walls and built additional defensive towers. The Normans held it for a long time but the Welsh, angry at losing a castle which they had originally built, recaptured it during the rising of 1294. Soon afterwards it was abandoned.

Three miles north-east of Abergynolwyn is Tal-y-llyn, considered by many to be the most beautifully situated lake in Wales. From this end of the lake you can run your car to pleasant picnic spots, but if you wish to fish a permit must be obtained. In the days when tourist traffic was much less than it is today, the local anglers considered it a poor day's sport if they returned home with fewer than a dozen trout. From the far end of the lake there is a path, but not an easy one, up to the summit of Cader Idris.

Beyond the outer walls of Castell-y-Bere lie the foothills of Cader Idris. The Welsh were wise in building their castle on a narrow ledge of precipitous rock which commanded two valleys. Edward I thought so too when, after a long and fierce assault, he took the castle and improved its defences (*Wales Tourist Board*)

Leaving Tal-y-llyn behind you, there is a long ascent of Bwlch llyn Bach to a point more than 600ft above the lake. From here the road squeezes a way between the mountains to reach a T-junction at Cross Foxes Hotel. From here there is a choice of routes: you can turn east, and after reaching a welcome car park and viewpoint at the top of the steep Bwlch Oerdrws you make an equally steep descent to Dinas Mawddy. From there you can either drive south on the A470 to Machynlleth or, on reaching the inn of the red-haired bandits, travel some twenty-five miles through the centre of Mid-Wales via the A458 to Welshpool. A short distance westwards from the Cross Foxes Hotel is Dolgellau, but whichever route you choose there is a scenic walk which should not be missed. Leave your car in front of the hotel and follow a stream to the 'Torrent Walk'. Along this walk the planners, with excellent taste, have provided viewpoints which will ensure your appreciation of the beauty of the river valley.

Dolgellau, in the Wnion Valley, lies in the shadow of Cader Idris, so for many years it has been the centre for those who find joy in clawing their way up to airy precipices. This riverside spot must have been known by the Romans who came here to search the surrounding hills for gold and silver. Because of its geographical position in the centre of radiating valleys the Normans did not consider it an ideal place to build a castle, preferring to erect their great fortresses along the sweep of Cardigan Bay, and on easily defended mountain crags. Owain Glyndwr had different ideas, for after establishing himself as a great Welsh leader, he made the town his capital and the site of his Parliament—although Machynlleth also claims that distinction (see page 135).

As a tourist centre it is one of the best in Wales. Places of great beauty surround the town; as mentioned above, there is the 'Torrent Walk', and also the 'Precipice Walk', a path encircling the mountains of Foel Faner and Foel Cynwch, towering above a lake whose waters hide the marble palace of a fairy king. Then there are the scenic routes up to the foot of Cader Idris, the home of giants and of Gwyn ap Nudd who hunted with a pack of fearsome hounds, ranging the mountain to seize the souls of those who fell from the steep scarps. No wonder it is said that 'to spend a night on Cader one lives on either as a madman or a bard'. The town has been described as 'a compact old-world town of narrow streets and small squares'. This is still true today for it has not altered much in three hundred years. It is a quaint little town, with crooked and meandering streets. Today's visitors sum it up as 'being a funny little place'. When the writer Thackeray stayed at one of the hotels he was not at all impressed with the service; feeling disgruntled he is reputed to have written:

> If you ever go to Dollgelly
> Don't stay at the Lion Hotel.
> You'll get nothing to put in your belly,
> And no-one will answer the bell.

From Dolgellau, drive across the Afon Wnion towards Llanell-ltyd, and just before you come in sight of the bridge over the Mawddach, a lane on the right will bring you to Cymmer Abbey. It was built about the same time that Owain Gwynedd, the great twelfth-century ruler of North Wales, set up his princely home at Dolgellau. The headless body of Llywelyn the Last was carried here from Builth in 1282 for burial. Today there is little to see, the riverside site being more picturesque than the ruins. Its treasure, reminding one of the past glory and importance of the ancient Cistercian abbey, is in the safe keeping of the National Museum of Wales at Cardiff. At the time of the Dissolution the monks buried the silver communion plate in the abbey grounds, determined to keep it out of the rapacious hands of Henry VIII. Centuries afterwards it was unearthed by miners digging for gold. Ever since Roman times gold has been worked in this district, and if you follow the Mawddach river for three miles to Ganllwyd you can visit their mines in the Brenin Forest. This lovely spot deserves to be known as Aber Eden, 'Vale of Eden', for the forest, and the rivers and waterfalls of the Afon Gamlan, flowing from the Rhinog mountains to join the Mawddach at Ganllwyd are nature's contribution to its beauty.

The tongue of land between the Mawddach and Wnion rivers, with the ruins of an abbey, ancient stones and forts, is full of history. Where the two rivers meet is Hengwrt whose owners, the Vaughans, gave the original text of the *Mabinogion* to the Welsh National Library at Aberystwyth. Some two miles north-east of Dolgellau, between Moel Cynwch and Foel Offrwn, is Nannau, a mansion which is the seat of the Vaughan family. It stands 700ft above sea level and has an interesting story which, in this part of Wales, is accepted as being more factual than fictional. There are several variations of this tale of the hollow oak tree which once stood in the centre of the park, but the one favoured by many local folk is that the tree concealed the body of David Gam after he had been slain by Owain Glyndwr. As the Welsh squire from South Wales was an opportunist and also a strong supporter of an English prince they probably feel that it was no more than he deserved. 'Glyndwr's Oak' did stand in the parkland, 'a broad and blasted oak, scorched by the lightning's vivid glare'. The historian Pennant gave a more reliable version of the incident, which is as follows. Hywel Sele, a cousin of Owain Glyndwr, had for a long time been at variance with the Welsh leader. One day they went hunting for game in the Nannau woodlands, but had not gone very far before they started to quarrel. Hywel, seeing a deer, took aim, but suddenly he turned and shot the arrow at the breast of his cousin who was saved by the armour which he was wearing beneath his cloak. Furious at such treachery Owain killed Sele and placed his body in the hollow trunk of a tree. For years Hywel's family and friends searched for him, but it was not until Glyndwr died that they were told of how and why Sele met his death. Madog, a close friend of Glyndwr, who was with him on that fatal day, led them to the tree which was split open to reveal a white skeleton. For years afterwards the local people feared to walk through the woods of Nannau at night.

The A496 road from Llanelltyd to Barmouth runs for about ten miles alongside the Mawddach estuary, recognised as one of the most scenic locations in Wales. It has been claimed that there is no view in the world better than the one up the Mawddach estuary, except the view looking down it. The mountain area north of the estuary was once called the 'California of Wales'. From the village of Bont-Ddu you can visit the Clogau gold mine and walk along the bank of a stream where the miners panned for gold. The Romans were hard taskmasters, and during the time they held the land between Dolgellau and Barmouth they rounded up the local people to labour in the mines. The interpretation of the word Dolgellau is 'Meadow of the Slaves'. Any unfortunate Welshman who laboured in the mountain caverns and felt the lash of a Roman whip would have agreed with this appellation. For the tourist the

Clogau mine is the most accessible, but other rich veins of gold were worked at Bedd-y-Coedwr, Vigra and Ogafu. It is traditional for Welsh mines to provide the gold used in rings for the Royal Family.

A glance at a good map (OS Dolgellau, Sheet 124) will show that from Bont-Ddu as far as Barmouth the road was engineered to run along a rock terrace on the lowest contour line of the mountains. At the mouth of the estuary a wooden bridge, an important part of the Cambrian Coast Railway, crosses it from Morfa Mawddach. When the railway bridge was built it was made wide enough to include a planked walkway, so that from the centre of the structure there is a magnificent view up the tidal estuary almost as far as Penmaenpool. From there the estuary narrows and twists, becoming the Afon Mawddach before passing Llanelltyd into the Vale of Ganllwyd. On the southern side the cloud-capped Cader Idris towers above the lower foothills between Penmaenpool and Arthog, an enchanting area where there are prehistoric remains and two small lakes.

Like Aberdovey, Barmouth with its sheltered land-locked harbour at the mouth of the estuary is a safe haven for ships running for shelter from storms in Cardigan Bay. Built on a narrow strip of land between the sea and the cliffs the town is just outside the estuary mouth. Above the main street the grey stone slate-roofed houses stand firmly on rising terraces of rock, secure but exposed to the full force of the gales sweeping up from the south-west. Barmouth has an air of solidity; it is not as attractive a place as Aberdovey, but is as good a tourist centre with a lot to delight and interest the holidaymaker. On the quay is the Yacht Club, the departure point for boats sailing up the picturesque Mawddach estuary or out into the bay.

Barmouth existed many centuries ago. Then it had the more appropriate name of Abermawddach, competing with Aberdovey as a port of trade. Tangible proof of its former importance can be seen in the ancient doorway of a house on the quay called Ty Gwyn. The original house was built to serve as headquarters for the Earl of Richmond, the young Welshman who became the first Tudor king of England.

In more recent years Barmouth was a place reputed to have provided a home and shelter for a Welsh sea-monster, a rival to

Nessie of Loch Ness. Sightings of a strange beast in the estuary have persisted for almost a hundred years, but such claims have been dismissed as defective vision bought about by imbibing too much Welsh ale. But since, on 2 March 1975, six perfectly sober schoolgirls saw it in daylight there have been second thoughts. A few years earlier, it was reported that three fishermen saw a similar creature in the Menai Strait.

Apart from Barmouth's seaside attractions there are splendid walks, all easily reached from the town. Along a 500ft high terrace above the sea is 'Panorama Walk'. The best time of day to take this airy walk is in the early part of the morning before the sun, at its noon-day height, causes the scarps of Cader Idris to project their shadows across the estuary; the side-lit precipices of the mountain are more dramatic before the sun has reached its zenith. In the light of early morning the beauty of the Mawddach estuary is at its best, the green fields at the foot of Cader Idris merging with the blue water, reflecting a mirror image of mountain and cloud. There is little wonder that this stretch of water running inland from the sea between the mountains is considered, by artist and poet, to be one of the most beautiful scenes in the world.

11

Between the Mawddach
and Traeth Bach

The Rhinog Mountains tower over the northern end of Cardigan Bay and the Lleyn Peninsula, an irregular range stretching between the Mawddach estuary and Traeth Bach, a landlocked haven of blue water tucked in the armpit of the peninsula. Hugging the coastline between Barmouth and Traeth Bach the Cambrian railway is in close company with the A496 road until it turns to run to the terminal station of Pwllheli, halfway along the south coast of the Lleyn Peninsula. From Barmouth, almost as far as Harlech the golden sands of the coast are crowded with holiday camps and caravan sites. This narrow exposed tract of land between the sea and the road will have little attraction for those in search of scenic beauty and places of historic interest.

A short distance northwards along the coast from Barmouth is Llanaber, a village with an exceptionally interesting church dating back to the early years of the eleventh century. Some claim that it is the finest example of Early English church architecture in Wales. The outside of the little church is not at all impressive, but inside the workmanship is unusually fine for this part of Wales. Students of architecture will find interest in seeing how the main architectural style developed from Norman to Early English. There are two ancient stones inside the church, one of which was once in use as a footbridge nearby and bears an inscription dating back to the tenth century. During the seventeenth and eighteenth centuries smuggling was an active and profitable business all along the extensive shoreline of Cardigan Bay, and one has the impression that the local people, particularly the inn-keepers, were on good terms with their friendly neighbourhood smuggler. The flat open coastline along this part of Cardigan Bay did not, unlike the rugged shores of Pembrokeshire with its hidden coves and caves, provide any safe hiding places where they could store their illicit goods. A local story claims that the smugglers used the table tombs in the churchyard to hide kegs of rum and brandy.

A little more than a mile north of Llanaber on the A496, a path on the right goes to another ancient ecclesiastical site. Many centuries ago Egryn Abbey overlooked Cardigan Bay, but now the site is occupied by a farm. Continue along the path and you will soon reach Carneddau Hengwm, an interesting burial-chamber of the Neolithic Age. This must have been one of the largest and most impressive barrows in Wales, for the long parallel heaps of stones suggest that there was a linked chain of burial chambers. From here another track going to the village of Talybont passes close to the hill fort of Craig y Dinas which still has some sections of the original stone walling. Nearby are the remains of a stone circle. The lower slopes of the Rhinog Mountains support a large number of stones and earthworks of prehistory, and a close study will reveal that the ancients aligned them in order to provide sighting points over the wild and trackless mountain wastes. The track, after crossing a stream, ends at another ancient memorial of the past, a large cromlech known as 'Arthur's Quoit'. From here a lane runs down to the main road, joining it near Llanddwywe.

Llanbedr is the next village northwards along the A496, a small place with stone cottages of pebble-boulder construction typical in this area of Wales. Inside Llanbedr church is an interesting spiral ornamentation which is found on some ancient stones, but more often in Ireland than in Wales. About one mile east of Llanbedr at Cefn Cymerean is a small Baptist chapel which was immortalised by the English painter Curnow Vosper in his picture *Salem*. If you are interested in collecting some unusual shells, a lane will take you down to a lagoon where two narrow strips of land almost touch to isolate it from the sea. The southern strip of land is called Mochras, but is more popularly known as Shell Island, where at least two hundred varieties of shell can be found. To the north of Llanbedr, standing on the very edge of the coast amid sand dunes is the ancient Llandanwg church, the mother church of Harlech. This isolated wind-battered sixth-century house of Christian worship must still be consecrated for services are held there.

From Llanbedr a narrow lane and the Afon Artro twist northeastwards through wooded valleys between Rhinog Fawr and Moel Goedog up to one of the most fascinating upland areas in

Wales; the way is wild and beautiful. When the film-makers searched for a mountain location similar to the frontier of India for filming *The Drum*, they came to the Rhinog mountains where they built pseudo-Indian villages and British forts. Elephants and Indian goats were photographed in Welsh *cwms*. Afterwards they left behind them a new breed of goats—distinctly Anglo-, or Welsh-Indian. Bandits roamed here long before the bogus Indian ones came to these Welsh hills, for at Drws yr Ymlid, 'The Door of Pursuit', a notorious bandit chief was caught and put to death by boiling. A fanciful story, but there may be some truth in it.

The hills close in, and the mountain track ends near a farm where you must leave your car, continuing on foot up Cwm Bychan to a lake. This was the way used by the Romans and medieval packmen to cross over the Rhinogs from Llanbedr and Harlech to Trawsfynydd where the Romans and, in later years, the Normans built a fort. Swinging away southwards from the lake the track ends at the foot of a series of roughly cut stone slabs, rising in five flights up to Bwlch Tyddiad. This rock staircase, marked on the maps as 'Roman Steps', is attributed to the Romans, but the way through the mountains must have been known and used by prehistoric man. After Roman usage, medieval traders probably set up the stone staircase to make the journey over the mountains less tiring. A short way from the top of the steps the track reaches the edge of a woodland where it joins several other paths which provide an easy descent to the main A470 trunk road to Trawsfynydd. From the edge of the wood an ancient way, also stepped and paved, goes through a *bwlch* and *cwm* to follow the Afon Cwmnantcot back to Llanbedr.

In the days when written history was embroidered with fanciful legend, Bran, a king of England, and his sister Branwen lived in a high castellated tower perched on a rock above the sea. The royal couple were no ordinary beings; they were the children of a sea-god who made sure that their tower at Ardllech was unconquerable. After Bran went to his particular Valhalla Welsh chieftains used the tower as part of their fort. What warriors could not do time and climatic erosion did, so when Edward I, the Norman castle-builder, saw the rock above the sea at Harlech he built on it one of the strongest castles in Wales. With the sea on one side and a 40ft wide rock ditch on the other it made a formidable fortress.

The defences of the castle were well tested when Madoc ap Llywelyn attacked it in the closing years of the thirteenth century. The castle proved to be too tough a nut to crack, and remained so until Owain Glyndwr tried to take it in 1404, but even he failed to breach the stout walls. For once, Glyndwr was patient, but it was only taken after a long siege when sickness and starvation reduced the garrison to twenty men. For the following three years Glyndwr lived there with his wife and family, but when he marched away to fight the Anglo-Normans in other parts of Wales he left it in the hands of his son-in-law Mortimer. On receiving news that the castle was being attacked Glyndwr brought an army back to Harlech, but failing to break through the besiegers it was forced to retire. The brave Mortimer fought well, and rather than surrender the fortress he starved to death. The garrison, now reduced in number, was overpowered by a force of a thousand men. Glyndwr's wife, his daughter and the four Mortimer children were taken prisoners and sent to London.

Harlech Castle was built by Edward I as part of his plan to ensure complete subjugation of the Welsh. During the Wars of the Roses it was held for the Lancastrians by Daffyd ap Einon. He refused to submit to Edward IV until he agreed that, 'with honour' Daffyd could march out of the castle at the head of his men. The famous Welsh song 'Men of Harlech' tells the story of these marching Welsh warriors

Prince Harry of Monmouth, elated after defeating the Welsh forces of Glyndwr in South Wales and again at Aberystwyth, was anxious for a final confrontation. The Welsh leader, dispirited at the loss of his castle and family, escaped his pursuers and hid amid the mountains he loved so much. Eventually the castle was recaptured by the Welsh, and during the Wars of the Roses it was held for eight years by Daffyd ap Einon, but even when the garrison was reduced to seventeen they were prepared to defend the castle until they too were killed. It was a long siege and Daffyd would only agree to surrender after receiving a promise that he and his men would be allowed to live. He was determined to have terms which were honourable, and sent a message to the English leader, saying

> in his youth he had maintained the defence of a castle in France until every old woman in Wales had heard of it, and in his age he would hold the castle in Wales so long that every old woman in France would know of it.

The English, honouring his bravery, allowed him to march out of the castle at the head of his men. The famous Welsh song, 'Men of Harlech', tells the story of these marching warriors.

The long history of battle and siege ended on the 10 March 1647 when the castle surrendered to John Jones, one of Cromwell's generals. John Jones, who married Cromwell's sister Catherine, lived in a secluded valley in the mountains above Llanbedr. When the Royalists re-established the English crown he was tried and executed as a regicide in 1660.

The view from the castle battlements will convince the tourist that he has reached the gateway to North Wales. Over the soggy foreshore of Morfa Harlech and Traeth Bach the heights of the Moelwyn hills are dominated by the peaks and crags of Snowdonia, and beyond the sunlit waters of Caernarfon Bay is the coastline of the Isle of Anglesey.

After exploring the historic castle a drive of about six miles will bring you to a spot where you can if you wish leave the main road and take a short cut across the Afon Dwryd over a toll bridge to Penrhyndeudraeth. If you continue along the A496 you will come to Maentwrog. The Afon Dwryd becomes narrow enough at Maentwrog for a bridge to allow a crossing to the north side of the river. Several roads meet here; turn left and you will soon be on the A487 road which runs along the south coast of the Lleyn Peninsula. However, if you continue on the A470 there is a delightful journey through wooded valleys to Betws-y-Coed. When you catch sight of the standing stone of Twrog turn sharp right along the lane to Llyn Trawsfynydd. Near the junction with a main road another lane will bring you to a particularly historic spot. The Romans built a fort here which is marked on the map as Tomen-y-Mur. They evidently considered this site on a spur of the Arenig group of mountains to be of prime importance, and as the period of their occupation lengthened they decided to add an amphitheatre. Not far south of the fort the straightness of the road to Llanelltud, near Dolgellau, suggests that it follows the line of a Roman road. There are traces of Roman military highways all the way from Conway in the north to Mawddach and on into South Wales. The Sarn Helen, named after Helen, the wife of the Emperor Maximus, is shown on many of the detailed OS maps of Wales.

As seen today, Tomen-y-Mur, 'The Mound of the Wall', is a mound on which the Normans, always appreciative of a good defensive position, built over the Roman fort, topping it with a high wooden palisade. There are records that William Rufus, 'the Red King', sought shelter here, and about 1118 King Henry I camped on the site. There are few places in Wales, especially lonely ones, which do not have substantial reminders of the prehistoric past. The stone of Maen Llwyd guards the west side of the Roman 'street' and on the east side is a 10ft high standing stone known as Llech Idris, after a giant who had his domain and throne on a high mountain above Dolgellau.

From Maentwrog, named after Twrog, a seventeenth-century saint whose memorial stone stands in the churchyard, another road will bring you to Ffestiniog, a village clinging to the hillside above a valley where the Ffestiniog narrow-gauge railway brings tourists up from Porthmadog. The reason for coming here, or at least one of them, is to take the Bala road as far as Pont-yr-Afon-Gam which, with estimable Welsh passion for meaningful place-names, could mean 'The Bridge over the Crooked River'. The falls of six separate cataracts along the river are worth seeing. Near the waterfalls of Rhaiadr Cwm is a second reason for this diversion.

This is an area of boggy ground, swirling mists and, of course, another mysterious lake. Most Welsh lakes have similar legends of fairy spouses who if admonished three times or touched by iron, will vanish. The story of Llyn Murwynion, 'the Lake of the Maidens', is refreshingly different, and is closely connected with another legend of a lonely spot called Beddau-gwr-Ardudwy, 'the Graves of the Men of Ardudwy'. Having heard the stories about the peerless beauty of the maidens living in the Vale of Clwyd the men of Ardudwy raided the valley and abducted prospective brides. The young men of Clwyd were furious. When they caught up with the raiders a ferocious fight took place which did not cease until every one of the abductors had been killed. The Clwydian maidens by this time had become completely infatuated by their captors, so rather than return home they ran into the lake and drowned themselves.

There are two places named Ffestiniog, but in order to avoid confusion one is known as Blaenau Ffestiniog. It is surrounded by quarries which supplied slates to all parts of the world. The slate town lies in the shadow of the Moelwyn and Manod ranges, mountains which have summits over 2,000ft above sea level. The streets, built of grey stone and slate-roofed houses, twist and turn through stacked piles of the waste from abandoned quarry workings. Some idea of the work of the slate miner can be obtained by a visit to the two slate museums in the town: Llechwedd Slate Caverns and Gloddfa Ganol Slate Mine. At both visitors may go underground and see the remains of spectacular workings, sometimes as cavernous as a cathedral nave.

Bridging a cleft in the mountains above the town is a concrete dam. As seen from the base of the mountains it looks unreal, giving the impression of being part of an outdoor set for a thrilling scene in a film. The dam is real enough, and when the contractors completed it to hold back the waters of a lake, an important part of a hydro-electric water supply, they filled in the deep ruts and resurfaced the steep winding road which had been constructed to bring building materials up to the dam. The site of this engineering wonder is at Tanygrisau, about a mile south-west of Blaenau Ffestiniog. From a pumping station at the lower reservoir it is possible to drive up the winding road to the new dam 1,000ft above the valley. From the upper reservoir, behind the dam, water rushes down the mountainside through large pipes to operate the turbines in the power station; the accumulated water in the lower reservoir is then pumped back to replenish the upper one. If you are nervous about driving up this exciting road there is a regular coach service from the centre of the town.

If you decide to take the short cut over the toll bridge, the road along the north side of the Afon Dwyrd is joined at Penrhyndeudraeth, but after returning from the two Ffestiniogs the river is crossed at Maentwrog. It is a pretty run through the woodlands bordering the north side of the river to Penrhyndeudraeth and the lowlands of Traeth Mawr to Minfford, from where a road southwards will bring you to a spot which might well be called 'Little Italy in Wales'.

About sixty years ago a Welsh architect, Clough Williams-Ellis, visited the little Italian coastal village of Portofino, and fell hopelessly in love with it. On his return home he explored the coast of Britain seeking a suitable place where he could build, in Italian style, a similar village. After a long search he found such a site near his own home; he called it Portmeirion. In fact this lovely site overlooking the waters of Traeth Bach was rediscovered, for it was first mentioned by Giraldus Cambrensis in 1188 when he wrote about 'the newly erected castle of Deudraeth built by the sons of Cynan'. When he designed and built the tall Campanile the architect acknowledged this historic fact, for on a tablet set in the base is the inscription:

This tower, built 1928 by Clough Williams-Ellis, architect and publican, embodies stones from the 12th century castle of his ancestor Gruffydd ap Cynan, King of North Wales, that stood on an eminence one hundred and fifty yards to the west

Situated on a tree-covered rocky bluff between the solid dullness of the castles built by the Normans at Harlech and Criccieth the village seems historically out of place. With gaily coloured houses set carefully around an old mansion, surrounded by trees and flowering shrubs, it cannot fail to fascinate the visitor. There are some who might even feel that it is too exuberant, a sort of manipulated Disneyland creation. One thing is certain—it proves that architecture can be fun. It was at Portmeirion that Noel Coward wrote *Blithe Spirit*, completing it in one week. The village has been used many times as a film set. Many who have stayed in this beautiful place will be sad to hear that last summer a disastrous fire gutted the hotel, and it is not certain if it can be restored to its former state.

Portmeirion stands on the south side of a short peninsula projecting into Traeth Bach. On the north side of the peninsula is the end of a causeway built across the mouth of the Afon Glaslyn. After paying a toll you can drive along the causeway to Porthmadog, a popular holiday and tourist centre. During the days when the slate industry flourished the harbour at Porthmadog was used for shipping Welsh slate to all parts of the world, and the narrow-gauge railway running alongside the causeway brought fully loaded trucks from the quarries in the Ffestiniog valley. The railway is still busy, but now it takes visitors on a scenic run through the Moelwyn hills, every mile a journey of breathtaking beauty. There is some uncertainty about the origin of the town's name. Local folk will tell you that it was from here that a Welsh

Built on a wooded hillside, the lovely Italianate village of Portmeirion overlooks Traeth Bach. Its creator, the late Clough Williams-Ellis, wished to build a coastal village resembling Portofino in Italy, and after a long search he found a suitable site for his 'Little Italy in Wales' (*Wales Tourist Board*)

prince, Madwg ap Owain Gwynedd, sailed to discover America three hundred years before Columbus, or that it was named after W. A. Madocks who reclaimed the marshlands about the town.

South of Porthmadog is Borth-y-Gest, a crescent-shaped village sprawling around a sheltered cove. After the busy streets of Porthmadog one feels that here is a place with a certain old-world dignity, deserving its description of being 'prim and pretty'. Unlike other places it is hardly ever crowded. To the west the sands continue round the headland of Garreg-goch to Black Rock, a favourite holiday beach and one on to which you can drive your car! There are some interesting caves at the end of the beach, and above them is a fine viewpoint overlooking Tremadog Bay.

Lying below the vertical cliff face of Allt Wen, 'White Cliff', is the village of Tremadog, taking its name from William Alexander Madocks who bridged the Glaslyn estuary with a causeway. The poet Shelley lived here for a while, becoming so keenly interested in this area of Wales that he supported Madocks' plan to reclaim the marshland above the causeway and helped him to organise the project. Shelley did little to make himself popular with the local people however, and after an attempt on his life by shooting he moved to another part of Wales. The story of this incident is that one night an irate farmer broke into Shelley's house and fired a pistol at him; missing the poet the farmer returned later in the night and tried again. The would-be assassin was never brought to justice, but it is generally supposed that he was a local farmer angry at the Englishman's habit of shooting any sheep which he found dying on the mountain. Another famous person was born at Tremadog in a house called 'The Woodlands'—he was T. E. Lawrence (Lawrence of Arabia), born here in 1888.

Tremadog's former town hall is now a craft centre while the former woollen mill is a laundry. South of the town is a nineteenth-century church and on the Porthmadog road there is a nineteenth-century porticoed chapel.

So far in this book our journeys have, in general, started from South Wales and along roads running from south to north. Many tourists from England would cross the Welsh border from Hereford, Shrewsbury or Chester. From all these border towns roads run from east to west into Wales. In the following chapter some of these lateral routes will be explored.

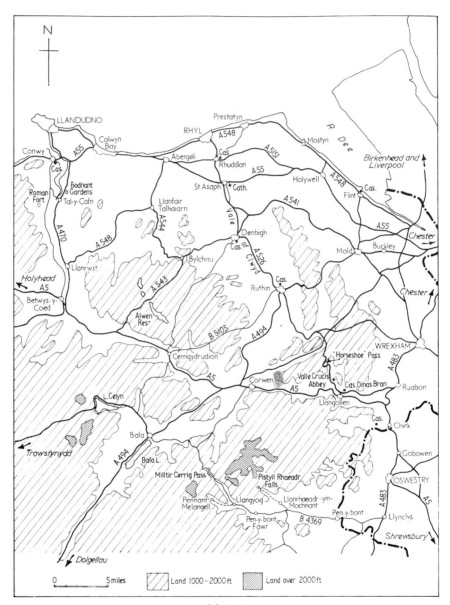

Map 11

The Central Marches
and the North-East

From Llandrindod Wells the main A483 trunk road is never far away from the eastern border of Wales. Passing through Newtown and Welshpool it slips across the border just before reaching the English town of Oswestry, returning into Wales to reach Wrexham. Nine miles from there it crosses the border again to the historic city of Chester, the northern gateway of Wales.

The main north-to-south road on the English side of the border is the A49 running from Hereford through Leominster, Ludlow, and Shrewsbury to Whitchurch. From the latter town the A41 goes on to Chester. All these towns are the main ones from where lateral roads branch off to run *across* the Welsh border, but as this book is about journeys *in* Wales the border road between Llandrindod Wells and Wrexham should be used!

There is a choice of roads from Newtown. Turn west and you can follow the A492 and A470 along the narrowing course of the Severn river to Llanidloes, then across the mountains to Aberystwyth. Another junction along the A470 will bring you to Machynlleth and Aberdovey. Newtown, in 1820, was called Drenewydd by the Welsh, and it was in that year that Roger de Mortimer decreed that a market could be held in the town. In the centre of an agricultural district where farm produce, good Welsh mutton and flannel was readily available the town prospered. There are accounts, however, of 'trouble at mill' and so, as at Llanidloes, a Chartist movement was formed. When the militia was sent in to deal with the angry, ill-paid workers they were pelted with stones. Being close to the English border some of the houses are of black-and-white timber construction.

The modern name of the town is most appropriate for it has been designated a New Town and a development area, so there are many new structures. The Textile Museum houses many exhibits of

Newtown's former life—old tools, machinery, etc. Glyndwr's Dolgellau parliament house stands in the Milford Road district, having been brought here in 1885. The Owen museum recalls Robert Owen, crusader for social reform, who was born here and is buried in the Old Churchyard. The new Church of St David contains an interesting memorial to the wives of Sir John Pryce.

A short way north of Newtown a minor road, the B386, goes to Montgomery, another town with a long history of trouble and strife. A mound marks the spot where a motte and bailey castle, Hen Domen, stood in 1092, one which was constantly attacked by English and Welsh. In the thirteenth century Hen Domen was superseded by a stone double enclosure castle nearer the town. It was a good day for the town when the castle was taken and dismantled by the forces of Parliament during the Civil War. Recent excavations have revealed much of the original structure. Several famous names are connected with Montgomery: Edmund Mortimer, the English son-in-law of Owain Glyndwr; Sir Richard Herbert and his son, Lord Edward Herbert of Cherbury, a brave soldier, diplomat and historian. Another son was George Herbert, the religious poet.

The next town to the west of Offa's Dyke, and in the shadow of the Long Mynd, is Welshpool—a town with an even more turbulent history of border warfare and cattle rustling. At one time Welshpool was the capital of the old kingdom of Powys; because of this it suffered more from warring factions than either Newtown or Montgomery. In addition to fear of devastation by both English and Welsh forces it was, and still is, liable to be inundated by Severn floods. The first castle here was built by Owain ap Gruffydd to halt the advance of the Norman Lord Marchers, so it is easy to understand that casual visitors were not welcomed. Today it is different, for now the castle is under the guardianship of the National Trust and is open to visitors. On the flower-bordered terraces can be seen the cannons which Clive, one of the ancestors of the Powys family, captured at Plassey in 1757. Inside the castle are to be seen many fine paintings, works of art and antique furniture. There are delightful formal gardens, also an orangery with eighteenth-century framed windows, surmounted with a balustrade bearing four lead figures of shepherds and shepherdesses.

Before the castle was built, the hills around the town supported prehistoric fortifications; on the Long Mynd, which means Long Mountain, there is Caer Digol, and on another hill is a fort known today as Crowther's Camp. When excavations were carried out some fine specimens of the tools and weapons of prehistoric man were unearthed.

Welshpool's parish church, St Mary of the Salutation, was founded in the thirteenth century and has been rebuilt and restored several times since. It owns a gold chalice dated 1662 which was in use until comparatively recently but is housed in the bank vaults nowadays. An attractive black-and-white cottage— Grace Evans' Cottage—has an interesting history connected with the 1715 Jacobite rising. The town has an ancient cockpit house where cock fights regularly took place. Two of Welshpool's more modern features are a small war memorial garden and a charming row of almshouses.

The English town of Oswestry is sixteen miles away along the A483, but two miles short of this 'foreign' town a lateral route over 'the roof of Wales' is available. On reaching Llynclys turn left along the A495 to reach the B4396 road towards Pen-y-bont and Llanrhaeadr-ym-Mochnant. If you have travelled from beyond the Welsh border it will soon become evident that you have entered Wales, for the place-names on almost every signpost start with double L's. It has been said that there are three qualifications needed for the correct pronunciation of Welsh words. You must have,

> A cold in the head.
> A knot in the tongue.
> A husk of barley in the throat.

If, after collecting the above, you still fail to impress the natives, you can cause discomfort by informing them that the surname of Jones is definitely bogus, and it will cause further embarrassment when you also assert that there is no letter 'J' in the Welsh language!

From Llanrhaeadr-ym-Mochnant you can visit one of the legendary wonders of Wales. Three miles away is Pistyll Rhaeadr, the highest and probably the most spectacular waterfall in Wales. It is easy to find—just follow the Afon Rhaeadr until the valley narrows to a rocky canyon. At the end of it is the fall, thundering down from the top of a 300ft high cliff into a deep pool; then, obscured by white spray, the torrent makes a repeat performance as it seeks a new outlet to fall another 50–60ft into a river pool. You cannot drive past the fall so it is necessary to return to the main road.

The next village along the B4396 is Penybont-fawr. Up to this point the route has, for Wales, been through reasonably flat pastureland between low hills. Now the way over 'the roof of Wales' begins to narrow, and as there are several sharp bends careful driving is essential. The road now squeezes a way through the foothills of the Berwyn Mountains, giving a foretaste of what is to come before Llangynog is reached. This village lies deep in the very heart of the Berwyns, and during the winter when the mountains are white with snow life must be very difficult. The relics of a railway terminus here are still recognisable. The village was once supported by slate quarrying and in the past the slate was transported by sledge. The beautiful landscape is pitted with disused quarries and lead mines, and the surrounding hills bear relics of Iron Age settlements.

When the mountain valleys were choked with swamp and dense undergrowth our ancestors made their way along trackways over the hills. Two such tracks still exist in this area, bearing the names of Ffordd Saeson and Ffordd Gam Elin. The latter means 'Helen's Winding Road', another reference to that mythical Romano–British lady who should have been the patron saint of road contractors and civil engineers. Through a narrow *cwm* a lane climbs up to the hamlet of Pennant Melangell, the hiding place of Monacella who, not wishing to marry, hid in this spot amid the Welsh hills. Unlike the materialistic Helen she was a saint, and when she died was buried in Pennant Melangell church. On the beam which once formed part of a screen inside the church are carvings which may confirm the truth of the strange legend of St Monacella's hares. They were known as Monacella's lambs, for if they sought refuge under her robe they were safe from huntsmen and their dogs. The saintly lady is supposed to be enshrined in one of the walls of the little church.

After leaving Llangynog the B4391 becomes steeper as it climbs between bare mountains which rise up to almost vertical crags. The top of the long incline is reached after driving along a narrow ledge cut in the flank of the mountain. This is the Milltir Gerrig Pass, and from it the road crosses a wide expanse of heather-clad moorland over 1,500ft above sea level, twisting and turning as it descends to Bala, the end of our journey over the roof of Wales.

The next tourist centre to be visited is Llangollen from where journeys can be made into north-east Wales, or across the mountains and moors through Corwen and Betws-y-Coed into Snowdonia.

From Llynclys, the starting point of our previous journey over the Berwyns across Wales, the route now travels northwards over the border on the A483 road, but slips back into Wales again at the boundary town of Chirk. Unlike so many castles which the Normans built along the line of the Welsh boundary, Chirk castle is habitable. Throughout the centuries after the Normans landed near Hastings one or another of the Mortimers are sure to appear on the scene. In 1310 it was Roger de Mortimer who flew his battle flag from the first stone keep on a mound at Chirk.

Although attacked many times the castle remained reasonably intact until the cannons of a Civil War onslaught breached the walls. When peace came the fortress was restored by Sir Thomas Myddleton, but during the ensuing years attempts to convert it into a luxurious home caused it to suffer almost as much from the over-enthusiastic restorers as from bombardment. The medieval windows have given place to large multi-mullioned ones which look completely out of place. The interior is far more interesting, having on display a four-poster bed where King Charles I slept and a pair of Cromwell's jackboots, while in several rooms fine pictures and furniture can be seen. The famous gates are considered to be wrought-iron artistry at its best.

Other battles took place in this border area. A short way from the castle, near Offa's Dyke, King Henry II and the Welsh fought a fierce battle, and had not Hubert de Clare flung himself in front of his royal master the king would have been killed by a Welsh arrow. The Welsh, facing strong English forces, had to retreat over the mountains to Corwen.

A section of the Shropshire Union Canal is to be seen at Chirk. A long tunnel opens into a basin from where the Canal is carried across the Ceiriog Valley, the railway viaduct running beside it.

About a mile north of Chirk the A5 road is forced to change

direction by the Dee river, running alongside it into Llangollen, one of the loveliest towns in Wales, situated in a delightful valley and surrounded by the wooded slopes of hill and mountain. To enter the main part of the town it is necessary to cross the Dee over a handsome bridge—a crossing which may have existed in the fourteenth century. The people of Llangollen are very proud of their bridge for it is regarded as being one of the 'Seven Wonders of Wales'. An old rhyme enumerates these as:

> Pistyll Rhaiadr and Wrexham Steeple,
> Snowdon's Mountain without the people,
> Overton yew-trees, St Winefride's Wells,
> Llangollen Bridge, and Gresford bells.

Since 1947 this lovely Deeside town has been internationally known as a centre of song and dance. For six days every year in summer the town is crowded with people who come to compete in an Eisteddfod. The competitors, gaily dressed in national costumes, throng the streets. In one short walk over the bridge you will meet happy people who have come from all parts of the world to sing and dance.

The fortress of Llangollen stands on a high hill above the town, and is marked on the map as Dinas Bran. It was probably built by Gruffudd ap Madog to provide quarters for a garrison from which his men could march to deal with any Saxon forces making their way through the valley of the Dee. As the castle is known as Dinas Bran, a more romantic theory is that it must have been built by the same mythical Bran who founded Harlech Castle. Whoever built it there is no doubt that it was a Welsh stonghold, and there is still enough of it left to convince the visitor that it must once have been an imposing structure. According to the *Mabinogion*, Bran was a King of Britain who had a cauldron with which, if he used the correct magical incantation, he could bring the dead back to life. As, according to legend, Bran was caught by his enemies and met his end by decapitation, obviously no magical rites were powerful enough to resuscitate him. His head was buried on 'a white hill overlooking the Thames', and as long as it remained there Britain was safe from invasion. When the Normans excavated the hill to lay the foundations for the White Tower of London Bran's skull was not unearthed. As their invasion was successful the old legend must have been true. Bran means crow, a bird which is related to the raven family, so the current legend which states that when the black ravens of the Tower of London fly away, the Norman fortress and Britain will fall, may be an updated legend to replace the one relating to Bran's head.

The famous 'Ladies of Llangollen' were two eccentric Irish spinsters who settled in the town in 1779. Of aristocratic background, they sported an odd, masculine style of dress, often being mistaken for respectable clergymen. They entertained many distinguished people, including the Duke of Wellington and Sir Walter Scott. Plas Newydd, their home, is open to the public.

Two main roads lead from Llangollen. One, the A5, goes west through Corwen to Betws-y-Coed and the mountains of Snowdonia; the A542 runs northwards towards Ruthin and Denbigh to the holiday resorts along the north coast of Wales. About two miles along the latter road are the ruins of Valle Crucis Abbey, once one of the main religious centres in Wales, and the burial place of Welsh princes. Some historians have claimed that Owain Glyndwr was buried at Valle Crucis but this has never been substantiated, although it is on record that he was last seen here by the abbot who, when the Welsh leader bade him a good morning, adding, 'you are about early good abbot', received the reply, 'nay, my lord Owain, it is you who are up early—a hundred years too early'. The abbot's comment was a wise one, for when the Tudors united England and Wales the amalgamation was approved by Glyndwr's descendants. Owain Glyndwr was never seen again and his place of burial is still uncertain.

Valle Crucis means 'The Vale of the Cross', and a short distance away is a mound on which stands the remains of a cross known as 'Eliseg's Pillar'. Eliseg was a Welsh prince who ruled this area during the eighth century. Cyngen, his grandson, erected the cross in memory of his grandfather who was killed in battle near Chester. The original cross was pulled down during the Civil War; when the mound was dug in 1779 to re-erect the cross, a skeleton was found and it was assumed to be that of Eliseg.

After leaving the cross the A542 twists into a horseshoe bend as it ascends the lower contours of Llantysilio Mountain; this bend is known as 'Horseshoe Pass'. During the summer months the sheep-cropped turf at the side of the road is lined with cars, their occupants picking the colourful gorse, feeding the sheep and admiring the view to the south through the Vale of Llangollen.

Next along our route is Ruthin, another town which suffered senseless destruction by Glyndwr—the fact that it was a Welsh town made no difference to him. It is considered a pleasant and interesting place; at least, George Borrow thought so. Another visitor, Walter Savage Landor, said, 'It is a pleasant town surpassing all I have seen and is nothing less than Heaven upon earth'. The castle, founded by King Edward I in 1281, withstood the attack of Glyndwr when he burned the town in 1400. What Glyndwr failed to do Cromwell accomplished when he tore down most of the structure, but after repair and conversion at the end of the nineteenth century it is now one of the most luxurious hotels in North Wales.

St Peter's Church at Ruthin was once a monastic foundation. The splendid oak roof of its north side was a gift from Henry VII as an expression of his gratitude for the support of the Welsh at Bosworth. The gates at the entrance to the Church were the work of R. and J. Davies, workers in wrought iron, who also made the gates for Chirk Castle.

An ancient limestone block, the Maen Huail, stands in the market-place. The grammer school and Christ's Hospital are Elizabethan foundations. Nantclwyd House is a fourteenth-century town house, tastefully restored. It has a splendid half-timbered front (exposed only in 1928) and a unique roof structure. Gabriel Goodman, Dean of Westminster in Elizabeth I's reign, is said to have been born here.

Legends are the spice of history, particularly those which have some tangible evidence to offer. There are two legends of happenings in this corner of Wales supported by the finding of artifacts which go a long way to proving their authenticity. The first relates that over the years strange and inexplicable patterns of light were seen moving about the castle grounds, also the figure of an armed man wearing only one gauntlet. When excavations were being carried out at the time of extensions to the hotel, a single medieval gauntlet was unearthed. The second legend concerns a mound at nearby Mold which was said to be haunted by a figure clad in gold. The mound was excavated in 1883 and in it was found a skeleton wearing a cape made of small segments of gold riveted to strips of leather. Scientific tests confirm that the cape, which is now in the British Museum, is at least three thousand years old.

The Normans must have considered this area of north-east Wales particularly important, for in it they built a chain of strong castles stretching from Llangollen—which had a ready-made Welsh castle—to Rhuddlan near the north coast. Eight miles north of Ruthin they built another fortress, at Denbigh, on a dominant site overlooking the Vale of Clwyd. Denbigh saw and suffered from as much military action as any garrison town near the Welsh border, and one soon becomes aware of its turbulent past. Before he was able to subdue and contain the Welsh, King Edward I had to build and strengthen the fortresses between Chirk and Rhuddlan. He had more than enough trouble at Denbigh, and it was not until he had finally dealt with Daffyd, the brother of Llewelyn the Last who had been slain near Builth Wells, that he was able to entrust the building of a castle to Hugh de Laci. This happened in 1282, but soon after the Norman masons completed their work the Welsh attacked and drove de Laci out of Denbigh. The castle was used in further actions during the Wars of the Roses and the Civil War.

Denbigh is a walled market town containing some interesting features: the remains of St Hilary's garrison church, dating from before 1334; the ruins of 'Leicester's Folly'—an unfinished church begun by Dudley, Earl of Leicester in 1579; the remains of an abbey destroyed by fire in 1898, originally a thirteenth-century Carmelite Friary founded by Sir John Salesbury—a gentleman who was reputed to have two thumbs on each hand. Several well-known if not famous people are associated with Denbigh; among them were Dr Samuel Johnson and the explorer H. M. Stanley who travelled across Africa in search of David Livingstone. Although Stanley worked in America and fought in the Civil War, he was born in Denbigh and brought up in a workhouse at St Asaph, a nearby town which has the smallest cathedral in England and Wales.

The last link in the chain of concentric Edwardian castles is northwards at Rhuddlan where it replaced an early motte-and-bailey fortress. The Norman castle, on a riverside site a short way from the sea, received goods and material from wharfs along the coast. King Edward I favoured this castle on the banks of the

Clwyd and he was probably there when news was brought to him of the birth of a son at Caernarfon Castle. Rhuddlan Castle, with others, was rendered untenable by gunpowder and cannon at the close of the Civil War.

If a few days at the seaside seem attractive, the north-coast resort of Rhyl is soon reached. It is a fairly new town but one of the most popular places along the coast with three miles of safe, sandy beach, a marine lake and many places of entertainment for the holiday-maker. To the east is Prestatyn, standing on a site which was occupied in Neolithic and Roman days. Not far away from the centre of this town Offa commenced his famous earthwork to determine, once and for all, the boundary between England and Wales. Behind the town the hills bear traces of prehistoric occupation and Roman mines. There is a choice of excellent holiday resorts along the coast—Colwyn Bay, Rhos-on-Sea and Llandudno. Less than a hundred years ago Colwyn and Rhyl were small fishing villages but now they are prosperous holiday towns with fine promenades and piers. Llandudno, despite its Victorian appearance, has a longer history than the others. The long curving bay stretching between two headlands, named by the Vikings who had settlements here as Little Orme and Great Orme, is lined with clean, well-preserved Victorian houses and hotels. The town is named after Tudno, a sixth-century saint who built his *llan*, or enclosure, on top of the Great Orme, but the ruins of hut-dwellings and a cromlech confirm that the headland was occupied long before St Tudno built himself a shelter on this wild wind-swept hill. Llandudno is not as noisy or as brash as the other coastal towns, which with their highly coloured stalls and raucous juke boxes are really miniature Blackpools. The attractions here have dignity, and nature has scooped out of the flank of the Great Orme a small amphitheatre which is known as 'Happy Valley'. It is a colourful glade where borders of Alpine and other flowers make a lovely show from May to September.

Llandudno is associated with *Alice in Wonderland*, as is evidenced by the memorial stone on the west promenade featuring a white rabbit consulting his watch. Charles Lutwidge Dodgson, better known as Lewis Carroll, resolved to write the story after spending a holiday here.

To the south, at the mouth of the Conway river, is Llandudno

Junction. From there the B5106 follows the river through the Vale of Conway to Betws-y-Coed, then, as the A5, it winds through the hills back to Llangollen. The lowlands on both sides of the river are covered with ancient relics, and the Carnedd range of mountains criss-crossed with ancient trackways and Roman roads. After about two miles a lane leads to Bodnant Gardens, famous for its displays of rhododendrons and other exotic flowers. There are azalea and magnolia spread around rock gardens and terraces. These beautiful gardens, open from spring to autumn, are among the best in Britain.

Our ancestors and the Romans considered it necessary to guard the passage through the valley to the Conway estuary; a short way down the valley road, at Tal-y-cafn, you can cross the river and visit the Roman fort of Canovium, then take a lane to a mountain track which soon reaches an Iron Age *caer*. Youth hostellers with a taste for ancient history will relish staying at the Youth Hostel here, for on the mountains they will find many ancient relics, also a burial chamber at the end of the Roman road coming from the coast through Bwlch y Ddeufaen, 'the Pass of the Two Stones'.

Where the valley narrows is situated Llanrwst, a busy little market town and once an assembly point for the cattle drovers. A picturesque three-arched bridge spans the river, and the date of its erection in 1636 is incorporated in a carving of the Stuart arms on the south side of the bridge. It is attributed to Inigo Jones but there is no conclusive evidence supporting this. The parish church is worth a visit for its magnificent rood loft which was brought from Maenan Abbey, but the pride of the church is the huge stone tomb of Llywelyn Fawr. There seems to have been some competition for the honour of providing his last place of rest as he was first buried in 1240 at Aberconway Abbey, then his tomb was removed to Maenan Abbey in 1283. At the time of the Dissolution he found rest at last in the lovely chapel at Llanrwst.

The next place southwards on the Conway river is Betws-y-Coed, an overcrowded, over-commercialised village, but the beauty of the river here with its falls and wooded glens is not easy to resist. It is claimed that there are more beauty spots to the square mile here than in almost any area in Britain. The fact that Betws is situated at the meeting point of three rivers—the Lledr, the Llugwy and the Conway—makes it an obvious tourist centre, a

173

Capel Garmon Burial Chamber is situated two miles south-east of Betws-y-coed. The impressive megalithic chambered tomb, a place of sepulture dating back to the beginning of the Bronze Age, still has one of the original immense roof slabs in situ

place of small cafés, guest houses, hotels and gift shops. The shops are filled with Welsh woollen shawls, trinkets, pottery and the usual tea-towels with highly coloured scenes of Betws—there are the Swallow Falls, the Fairy Glen and the Miner's Bridge in glowing colours. If you wish to get away from the overcrowded river banks and falls there are walks through green woods along less-crowded streams, backed by hills concealing sites of historical interest.

In a wooded valley at the foot of Moel Siabod are the ruins of a castle which was the last in Wales to be taken by King Edward I. The fortress of Dolwyddelan was built by the Welsh long before the Normans came to Wales, and some claim that defensive works of some kind existed here as early as AD 500. Sited near medieval tracks and a Roman road it must have seen a great deal of fighting, for the Welsh when not fighting the Anglo-Normans were easily roused to fight among themselves. Times were hardly ever peaceful. One Welsh chieftain who came here to seek peace and quiet is reported as saying, 'If I stay at my house in Eifonydd I shall either kill my own relatives or be slain by them.' It was a soldier's world, and to be proficient in the use of weapons ensured a longer span of life. As a matter of historical interest you can see inside a church at Betws-y-Coed the tomb of a *Welsh* knight who fought for an *English* king at Bosworth. North of the A5 highway is Capel Garmon where there is one of the largest and most impressive chambered burial tombs in Wales. This long barrow place of sepulture, dating back to the beginning of the Bronze Age, still has one of its immense roof slabs *in situ*.

Cerrigydrudion, eastwards along the A5 from Betws-y-Coed, is a small village whose name evokes memories of past battles—for it means 'the Rock of the Brave Men'. On a hill to the south of the main B4501 road to Denbigh is Caer Caradog. To the Welsh this is a hill of shameful memory, for it was here that Cartimandua, Queen of the Brigantes, betrayed Caractacus to the Romans who were pursuing him after he had been defeated by Scapula in AD 51. North of Cerrigydrudion is the Alwen reservoir. Corwen lies southeastwards along the A5 and is the entry to the valley of the Dee. This typical Welsh market town was a favoured rally-point for the Welsh troops of Owain Glyndwr, and here he left his mark. Owain was never one to suffer fools gladly, for he was an impatient fellow and unable to accept other opinions on points of military strategy. One day, angered at being opposed by some of his followers, he threw his dagger from a hillside above the town towards the church. If you examine the lintel over the south doorway you will see that it is marked with a cross, the long arm of which is narrowed to a dagger point. It was at Corwen in 1789 that the foundations of the National Eisteddfod were laid, when the support of the London Welsh Society and the foremost Welsh bards was obtained by a Corwen man, Thomas Jones, for an eisteddfod held at the Owain Glyndwr Hotel.

There are the remains of several fortifications on the hills around the town. One of them, Caer Drwyn, is the largest, and may have been used by Glyndwr. Near this spot, at the foot of Llantysillo, is a house known as Glyndwr's Palace.

Llangollen lies eastwards of Corwen along the A5 road.

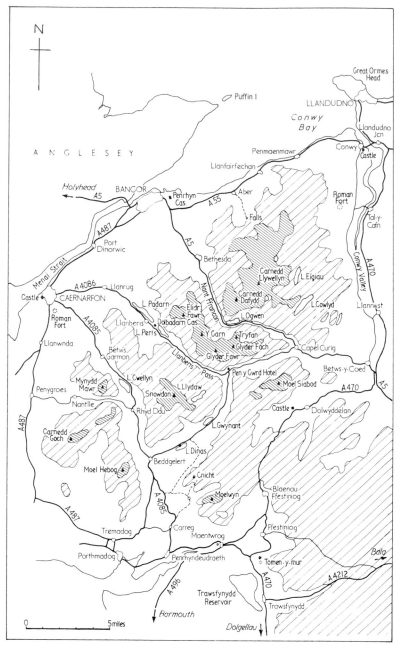

Map 12

13

Snowdonia and the North Coast

From Porthmadog there are two routes to Beddgelert, a small village at the junction of two valleys separated by the mountains of Snowdonia. One road, the A498, from Tremadog Square climbs between the foothills of Moel Ddu, Moel Hebog and the Aberglaslyn river; another route, the A4085, running parallel, starts from Penrhyndeudraeth and leads to Garreg, where one becomes very aware of the enchantment of the Welsh mountains. Just beyond Garreg a lane on the right goes to Cnicht, a mountain known as 'the Matterhorn of Wales'. The lane ends when it reaches the small hamlet of Croesor; from there, if approached from the right direction, the mountain is not difficult to climb, and is well worth the effort.

Croesor is on the line of an ancient trackway. Between the northern end of the hamlet and Bwlch Wernog are traces of a stone pavé laid down by our ancestors long before the Romans came to Britain. The Romans used this as a base for their road from the fort of Segontium at Caernarfon to another at Tomen-y-mur near Trawsffynydd, then over the mountains to South Wales. At Bwlch Wernog the trackway reaches a lane coming through the Nant-moor valley from Nant Gwynant and the southern buttresses of Snowdon. If, not so many years ago, you had come through this hidden valley the sight of an oriental village and the high-pitched chatter of a language strange to this part of Wales would have been perplexing. When the film-makers made *Inn of the Sixth Happiness* they built with stick, canvas and matchboard a pseudo-Chinese village; then, for further realism, they flooded some low-lying fields to create the only rice paddy fields in Wales.

At Aberglaslyn the roads from Tremadog and Penrhyndeud-raeth are briefly joined together by a picturesque stone bridge, spanning a deep gorge through which the Afon Glaslyn rushes down from the top of Nant Gwynant to Tremadog Bay. In the nineteenth century this spot was called Aber Glaslyn, meaning 'the mouth of the Glaslyn', for before the causeway at Porthmadog and tidal sluices were constructed to hold back the sea, the Afon Glaslyn was wide and deep enough for small ships to sail up the river from Tremadog Bay.

North of the old bridge is the Aberglaslyn Pass, a *bwlch* famous for its beauty. Road and river now twist their way through the wooded pass to Beddgelert. As you enter the village you will see the Goat Hotel whose former owner made sure that even if the name of Kelert, an early saint, was forgotten, the name of the village would be remembered as the home of Gelert, the brave hound who saved his master's child from being devoured by a wolf. The old legend of brave Gelert may be founded on an actual happening, but it cannot be proved that it took place here, or that the *bedd* (grave) which the hotel owner set up in a nearby field is that of Gelert. The story tells of how Prince Llywelyn returning to his lodge after hunting found his hound Gelert spattered in blood, and the cot of his infant son overturned. Hastily assuming that the dog had attacked the child he killed it, only to find afterwards that his son was unharmed, lying near the body of a wolf which the faithful dog had killed in rescuing the infant.

A story about the Goat Hotel might have more truth in it, and this too is connected with Mr Pritchard, the owner of the hotel who created Gelert's grave. If you stay at the hotel and wish to spend a peaceful undisturbed night, avoid room number twenty-nine. The ghost of the hotel owner is said to have appeared to a servant girl who used this room, telling her to give a message to his widow that she was to look under the hearthstone of the bar fireplace. When the stone was removed a treasure trove of gold coins was found. This bar-room is now used as a gents' toilet.

Beddgelert is beautifully situated at the junction of three valleys and two rivers. The Afon Glaslyn, noisy and boisterous, rushes through from its source on the southern side of Glyder Fawr. Almost every mountain in Snowdonia has been a hiding place for fugitives. When Owain Glyndwr sought concealment from his enemies he found a cave above Beddgelert on Moel Hebog. If you have sufficient energy to climb the mountain you can find it there today. It is clearly marked on the Ordnance Survey maps.

After crossing the Afon Glaslyn there is again a choice of routes. The A4085 goes direct to Caernarfon, and the A498 through Nant

Gwynant to the top of the Llanberis Pass, or on to Capel Curig, through Nant Francon to Bangor. Just less than four miles along the Caernarfon road is Rhydd Ddu where a left-hand turn, between Llyn-y-Gader and Llyn Byware, goes through the beautiful Nantlle Valley to Penygroes. From Nantlle there is an unforgettable view back through the valley to the foothills and summit of Snowdon. The road ends at Penygroes, which was an important place before the end of the slate industry. To the north-east stands Glynliffon, a nineteenth-century mansion, now a college.

Except for a few cottages and an inn there is not anything of interest at Rhydd Ddu. It is better known as a starting point of a track, which joins another one coming from Beddgelert, to the summit of Snowdon. The final section of the mountain track runs along the edge of the precipice of Lliwedd as it ascends steeply to the summit. When the ridge of Clogwyn du'r Arddu is reached there is an awesome drop, so walkers must proceed with care. Further north, at Betws-Garmon, is the garden of Nantmill. A notice invites you to leave the road and wander freely round the gardens where there is a pretty stream and waterfall. Another notice draws attention to the rocks at the side of the waterfall where you can see the small elvers attempting to scale the slimy rocks.

Both roads leading from the end of the bridge at Beddgelert are worth taking, but the most interesting one runs through Nant Gwynant up to the junction with the A4086 at Pen-y-Gwryd. After about one mile a path leaves the main road and climbs through a wood to Dinas Emrys where the scant remains of a tower are all that is left of the twelfth-century castle which the Welsh built to guard the southern end of the Gwynant valley. Almost opposite, on the other side of the valley road, is Llyn Dinas, a lake which must have provided piscatorial delicacies for the occupants of the castle; it is appropriately named 'the Lake of the Fortress'.

If you have come through the Nantmoor valley the main A498 road is reached near Plas Gwynant, where there is the start of another Snowdon mountain track. This track winds through Cwm-y-Llan up to the cliffs of Lliwedd. A short way up the *cwm* is Plas-cwm-Llan where the late Sir Edward Watkins, the pioneer of this track which bears his name, once lived. A little further on is a large boulder with a plate set into it, marking the spot where Prime Minister Gladstone addressed a large crowd. It has been claimed that he afterwards climbed as far as Lliwedd, but as he was then eighty-three years old this is hardly likely.

About four miles from Beddgelert the road runs alongside Llyn Gwynant, a lake fed by the Afon Glaslyn on its way down from the Glyders where it collects the watershed from the slopes of Gallt-y-Wenalt, a rocky buttress at the base of Lliwedd. From the end of the lake the road makes a steep ascent. Just before reaching the top of the valley there is a convenient pull-in on the left of the road, an essential stop for the keen photographer and anyone interested in fine scenery. From this high viewpoint the two blue lakes and the road curving a way between the mountains back to Beddgelert combine to present one of the finest scenic views in North Wales.

In no great distance the top of Nant Gwynant is reached, and there the road reaches a T-junction, one arm going east at the foot of Moel Siabod and the other into the Pass of Llanberis. At the junction is the Pen-y-Gwryd Hotel, used since the mid nineteenth century as a centre for mountaineers. In the early 1950s the team who defeated Everest stayed at the hotel, practising their climbing amid the snow-clad peaks of Snowdonia. After reaching the summit of Everest in 1953 they held a reunion at the hotel, leaving a piece of the summit rock on which is inscribed: TO MY OLD FRIENDS CHRIS AND JOE BRIGGS, EDMUND HILLARY and the word, EVEREST ROCK. The ceiling of one room has been autographed by Hillary and other famous mountaineers.

At the top of the Llanberis Pass, backed by the heights of Glyder Fawr and Glyder Fach, is the Pen-y-Pas Youth Hostel, a convenient centre for walkers and climbers. Two walking routes start from the car park opposite the hostel; the Miner's Track, once used by the miners who worked in the copper mines at the base of Snowdon, and the PYG Track. This strange name may have an association with the shoulder of Bwlch Moch which it crosses. Moch, of course, is the Welsh word for pig.

The Miner's Track, which eventually joins the PYG Track, is the most interesting, but as a lake has to be crossed over a stone causeway, this route is only possible after a sustained spell of dry weather. The first part of the track up to Llyn Llyddaw is quite wide, but after crossing the lake it narrows. From this point, owing to erosion caused by years of use, it sometimes becomes necessary for the walker to determine the correct direction by looking ahead

View of Grib Goch from summit of Snowdon. The most interesting walkers' track up the mountain is the PYG track which starts from the top of the Llanberis Pass. This photograph, taken from the summit of Snowdon, shows the track winding along the flank of Grib Goch

for the cairns which line the track. From Llyn Llyddw is a steep climb until the track joins the PYG Track which takes a fairly easy way along a contour line to the blue-green tinged waters of Llyn Glaslyn. The word *glas* means both blue and green in Welsh, so the lake, tainted by the copper waste from the old mines, is suitably named. The track, seeking the easiest gradient, zig-zags a way between the cairns to the top of a ridge, meeting the Snowdon Mountain Railway and the walker's track which follows it up from Llanberis. To reach the summit from here takes only about eight or ten minutes.

The Welsh mountains have attracted tourists for centuries, especially during the Napoleonic Wars when it was not possible to travel on the continent of Europe. It was at this time that artists, poets and writers discovered the beauty of British scenery, particularly in Wales and the Lake District. George Borrow, after reaching the summit of Snowdon, wrote a vivid and factual account in *Wild Wales*, of what he was able to see.

There we stood, enjoying a scene inexpressibly grand, comprehending a considerable part of the mainland of Wales, the whole of Anglesey, a faint glimpse of part of Cumberland, the Irish Channel, and what either might be a misty creation or the shadow outline of the hills of Ireland.

Although the mountain scenery is undoubtedly grand another writer, the Reverend W. Bingley who toured this area in 1797 was more impressed by the Welsh women. He wrote,

Mary Morgan having mislaid her door key often entered her cottage by climbing the slates and descending the chimney.

He also admired the aged Margaret Uch Evans, and wrote of her that she,

Rowed well, played on fiddle and harp, and at the age of seventy she was still the best wrestler in the country . . . She was a blacksmith, shoemaker and boatbuilder!

The A4086 emerges from the confinement of the mountains at Llanberis, and from there the easy way to reach the summit of Snowdon is by taking the mountain railway. Opposite the Llanberis railway station the thirteenth-century fortress of Dolbadarn stands on a rock-knoll between Llyn Peris and Llyn Padarn. The tower-keep once held two important prisoners. Prince Llywelyn Fawr held his brother, Owain Goch, there for twenty years, and after a battle in 1401 Owain Glyndwr used it to imprison Lord Grey of Ruthin. Above the two lakes the largest pumped-water storage scheme in Europe is nearing completion, and you can visit a museum which shows how the quarries of Llanberis were worked to supply slates which were sent to all parts of the world.

The name Caernarfon conjures up a mental picture of a multi-towered fortress guarding the mouth of the Afon Seiont, a site of great importance where the British built their fort of Caer Seiont. When the Romans, led by Julius Agricola, fought their way to this corner of north-west Wales they built their fort of Segontium on a new site just outside the centre of the town. Unusually, they did not make use of the ready-made site at the mouth of the river but after capturing it from the Welsh they probably strengthened and used it as a barbican, considering that the old fort would take the

initial assault from attackers sailing down the Menai Strait. The
building of the new fortress began about AD 78. The Romans first
erected a strong wooden palisade and surrounded it with a high
bank of earth, then about twenty years later Trajan, and Hadrian,
who had previous experience in building walls, commenced re-
building Segontium in stone. It was excavated in the early 1920s
and the artifacts which Sir Mortimer Wheeler unearthed are
displayed in a small museum built next to the Roman remains.

The Welsh, as many memorials of the past suggest, have always
resisted domination by action and volubility. Standing on a
pedestal above the square at Caernarfon, near the great walls of the
Norman castle built by King Edward I, a gull-splashed Lloyd
George raises his bronze fist. Could he be objecting to the castle-
builder's ploy that he kept his word when he showed his baby son
to the Welsh as 'the native-born prince who could speak no
English'? It suggests that the Norman king as well as being a
formidable soldier was also a good politician, for a similar
presentation of the heir to the throne is enacted at the castle today.
In 1911 the late Edward, Duke of Windsor, was invested there by
his father King George V, as Prince of Wales; on 26 July 1958
Queen Elizabeth II promised that her son Charles, as Prince of
Wales, would be presented to the Welsh people at Caernarfon
Castle. This investiture took place in 1969.

When Edward I reached the mouth of the Seiont he approved of
the ancient site which by then had a motte and bailey castle. In the
summer of 1283 the building of the mightiest castle in North Wales
commenced, and was completed by Edward's son who, in 1327,
died from torture in a dungeon at Berkeley Castle near Gloucester.
Glyndwr made several determined attacks on the castle, and so
afraid were the English that their enemies might find some way of
entering the fortress that it was decreed that no Welshman was
allowed to stay inside the town walls after sunset. After Henry
Tudor won the crown of England he passed a law in 1507 which
allowed his fellow countrymen free entry and complete residence
at any time. During the Civil War the castle changed hands several
times, but in 1660, 'concerning it to be for the great advantage of
ourselves and posterity to have the Castle of Caernarfon and the
strength thereof demolished', the local dignitaries arranged to
have it pulled down, but because of the enormous cost complete

demolition was never achieved, so the fortress, town walls and gateways remain almost intact.

Northeast of this historic town is Port Dinorwic. In the days when the quarries in the Llanberis valley were busy a light railway brought slates to the quayside for shipment abroad. One of the Dinorwic ships, the *Mary Mitchell*, was used during the First World War as a decoy to attract the attention of German submarines. When a U-boat surfaced in close range of the ship, the concealed guns gave it a hot reception and usually sank the German raider. These ships were known as 'Q' ships, and the *Mary Mitchell* was particularly successful. To the north-west of the port lies the park of the eighteenth-century Vaynol Hall.

From Port Dinorwic the A4087 road turns inland from the Menai Strait to Bangor, reaching the coast again at Conway Bay. A university and the modern restoration of an ancient monastic church are Bangor's main buildings. Bangor Cathedral was founded before Canterbury, for there was a church there in the sixth century. Despite being battered by Norman and Welsh leaders a fair amount of the original stonework remains, and inside there are several monuments connected with the past. Near the cathedral is a unique garden of bible-mentioned flowers. Bangor is a convenient centre for exploration of the coast from the Menai Bridge to Conway and Llandudno. Cross over Telford's fine suspension bridge and you can explore Anglesey, the kingdom of the Druids, a land as rich in legend and history as any other part of Britain. The Tudor lineage sprang from this green island where their ancestors were content to till and farm the land.

South of Bangor is Llandegai where the A5 trunk road enters the Nant Ffrancon valley, wriggling a tentative way between the Glyder and Carnedd mountains. Three miles away is Bethesda where the deep terraced slate quarries of Penrhyn supplied material to roof many of Britain's finest houses from the time of Queen Elizabeth I. Below this slate village the landscape becomes wilder, and high craggy precipices cast dark shadows over the valley road. The highest crag, Carnedd Llywelyn, is only 74ft less in height than Snowdon. After rounding the shoulder of Craig-ddu, Llyn Ogwen is reached. If you should wish to scale other Welsh mountains there are tracks up to the pyramid-shaped Tryfan and the even loftier summits of Glyder Fach and Glyder

Fawr. Enclosed in a natural amphitheatre of rock at the foot of
Glyder Fawr is Llyn Idwal, and a cleft in the cliffs behind the lake
is Twll-ddu, 'Black Hole', perhaps better known to climbers as the
'Devil's Kitchen'. From Llyn Ogwen the A5 curves down the
valley to Capel Curig, meeting the roads coming from the
Llanberis Pass and Betws-y-Coed.

Near Llandegai, between the Afon Ogwen and Bangor, is
Penrhyn Castle, with sham medieval towers overlooking Conway
Bay. Lord Penrhyn built this castle, designed by Thomas Hopper,
between 1827 and 1840, choosing the site of one built by a Welsh
prince in AD 720. The present castle is built of the finest material,
and inside much of it is in Norman style. The great hall with its
rich carving in stone and wood is very impressive, other rooms
containing many original furnishings, including a massive four-
poster bed made of slate from the Penrhyn quarries. One part of
the castle is used to display a collection of old locomotives, and
another room contains dolls from many parts of the world. The
castle and the beautiful gardens are open to visitors throughout the
summer months.

The next river outlet into the sea is about five miles away where
the Afon Aber, after forcing a way through a narrow rent in the
Carnedds, finds a less resistant passage across the Lavan Sands
into Conway Bay. At Aber the passage from the bay is guarded by
an ancient *caer* and a castle mound. This small green mound
represents a spot which played an important part in the history of
Wales. It was here that Llywelyn ap Gruffydd, the last native
Prince of Wales, had his castle, a fortress he refused to leave when
summoned in 1282 to Rhuddlan Castle to make obeisance to King
Edward I. This incident angered the English king, causing him to
accelerate his plans for the complete conquest of Wales.

About fifty years beforehand, Prince Llywelyn Fawr, related by
marriage to another king of England, showed his contempt for
Norman power and treachery. At a battle which took place near
Montgomery he captured the powerful Norman William de
Braose, and held him to ransom at Aber Castle. Llywelyn treated
his prisoner well, allowing him reasonable freedom within the
walls of the castle—too much it seems, for de Braose carried out a
romantic intrigue with Llywelyn's wife, who was the daughter of
King John. When the Welsh prince discovered this he hanged the

Norman on a nearby hill. His wife, who was fascinated by de Braose, is supposed to have been asked by a friend what she would give for a sight of her lover. Her reply was that she would willingly surrender 'Wales, England and Llywelyn to boot'. When her husband was told of this he led her to a window from which, to her horror, she saw the body of her Norman lover hanging from a tree.

From Aber you can walk through one of the most beautiful glens in Wales to the waterfall of Rhaiadr Mawr, more commonly known as the Aber Falls. The fall of white water cascading down from a height of 180ft is more impressive if visited after a few days' rainfall. To reach it proceed along a lane for about three-quarters of a mile, then take a track along the west side of the Afon Aber for about one mile.

Prime Minister W. E. Gladstone loved North Wales and spent several holidays along the coast a few miles east of Aber. Llanfairfechan and Penmaenmawr were two places he favoured, and he probably enjoyed walks in the hills overlooking Conway Bay. If interested in antiquities the remains of an ancient British settlement would have intrigued him, and by the roadside near the small village of Garreg-fawr he would have seen a Roman milestone. Among these hills above Conway Bay is abundant evidence from which to conjure up pictures of the distant past. Alongside the tracks of the Carnedds are standing stones, the guide-posts of early man, and in the centre of a Druidical circle archaeologists discovered an urn containing the cremated remains of a child together with a bronze knife which may have been used in some nauseous rite of bloody sacrifice. Industry, too, is represented, for among these mountains there is the site of a Stone Age factory where axes were manufactured.

From Penmaenmawr there are two roads to Conway, either the coastal road, the A55, which tunnels through the obstructive rock headland of Penmaen-bach Point, or by way of the Sychnant Pass. To the tourist the latter route is more interesting, and he will enjoy taking this road over the Conway Mountain. Careful driving is necessary, for part of the way is along steep, airy turns which run close to the edge of high precipices, but there is compensation in the magnificent scenery and views.

Conway, surrounded by massive stone walls, has been called the Welsh Carcassonne; with its great castle, in Norman times it must have been the most well-protected town in Britain. The road coming down from the Sychnant Pass ends at one of the town gateways. When Edward I was crowned the English were not doing too well in North Wales, their early fortresses and military outposts often failing to hold back the Welsh. However, when the English king carried his standard into North Wales they were forced to submit, and the castles which the Normans built on carefully selected sites played an important role in holding them down. The grey multi-towered fortress of Conway is only second in importance to Caernarfon in the chain of castles which Edward I built in North Wales. As the walls of Conway were rising above the riverside site other Norman fortresses were being built; in fact, within a period of eighteen years the Norman masons, with conscripted labour, completed ten castles. To establish complete command and subjugation of the Welsh King Edward built

Conway, with its Edwardian castle and massive town walls, has been called 'The Carcassonne of Wales'. The multi-towered castle forms an important link in the chain of fortresses which Edward I built in North Wales. Dominating the Conway Estuary it took, from 1277, but five years to build. It is an outstanding example of a medieval fortress, as fine as any in Europe

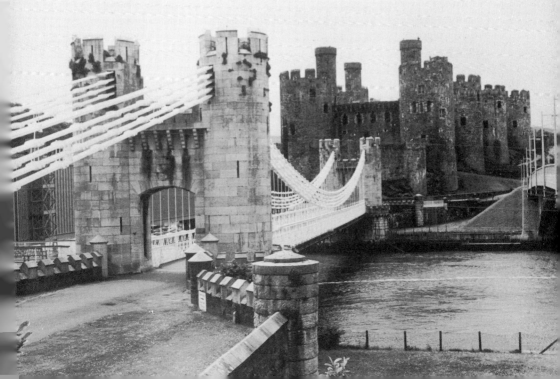

quickly, so that the castle he needed to dominate the Conway estuary took, from 1277, but five years to build, and the town which grew around it was enclosed by high walls with towers and gateways.

The invaders, despite the formidable defences, were never left in peace; the Welsh, always quick to seize an opportunity, seeing that the high tide in the estuary had flooded the land around the castle, made sure that provisions could not be taken there by boat, and at the same time ensured that nothing could be floated over the flood-water which inundated the landward side of the fortress. Their siege was unbreakable, compelling the king and garrison to eke out a sparse existence on rations of 'salted meat and coarse bread, with water mixed with honey for drink'. Their victory, causing discomfort and hardship to the Normans, was moral but not lasting, for when the floods receded the Welsh retired to the safety of their encampments in the surrounding hills.

There was little the Normans could do to avoid such inconvenience, and in 1399 another king of England suffered similar discomfort at Conway, but the outcome was less fortunate. It was then, after landing on the Welsh coast from Ireland, that King Richard II took refuge behind the castle walls. Such was the condition of the building that he found little comfort there and not much food—but after betrayal and capture by Bolingbroke he cound conditions even worse when confined in a prison tower at Flint.

It was inevitable that Owain Glyndwr, unable to stomach this English intrusion, made an attack on the castle, and for a time he was the self-appointed lord of the fortress, but the dignity and impregnability of this Norman lair ended at the conclusion of the Civil War. After the Restoration King Charles II gave the Earl of Conway permission to dismantle the castle, probably remembering that it was one which caused his father more than enough trouble in the Civil War. The Earl had plans to use the lead, timber and other materials to build himself a fine residence in Ireland, but the vessel he chartered to ship the material across the Irish Sea sank during a storm.

Despite this, and later vandalism, the castle is still attractive and of interest to the tourist as an outstanding example of a medieval military building as fine and elegant as any in Europe. The town, too, is full of interest with many ancient houses where architectural features and date-stones confirm the date of origin. There is the Tudor mansion of Plas Mawr where displays of art and local crafts are held. The house with carved gables, elaborate plaster ceilings and fireplaces show the expertise of the Elizabethan builders. On the corner of High Street and Castle Street another timbered building claims to be the oldest dwelling in Conway, and a house on the quay justifies its claim to be the smallest.

Despite wars, siege, the passing years and the insensitive efforts of the despoilers, the walls of Conway enclosing the historic castle still stand as a reminder of the exciting events of bygone days. Telford's early nineteenth-century suspension bridge, built almost six hundred years after the castle, looks almost part of the original fortress.

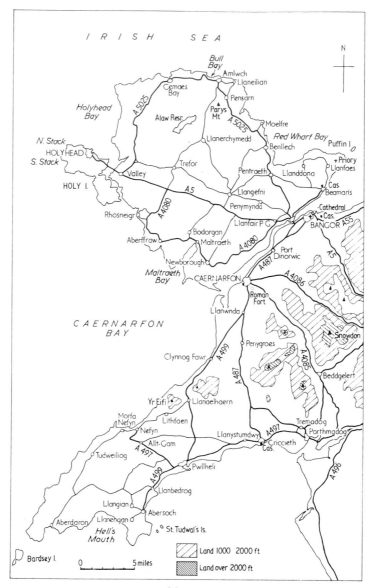

Map 13

14

Anglesey and the Lleyn Peninsula

Three miles south-west of Bangor is the narrowest crossing point along the Menai Strait between the mainland and the island of Anglesey. Nowadays the passage is easy and certainly less hazardous than when Paulus Suetonius and his cohorts assembled to cross the narrow channel to deal with the Druids. This first attempt in AD 61 was only partially successful, for it was seventeen years later that another army, led by Agricola, finally wiped out the high priests of Mona. The main centre for the fanatical cult of Druidism was at Mona, now known as Anglesey, and as these white-garbed priests were largely responsible for providing religious incentive to Welsh resistance the Romans were determined to destroy their sacred groves and temples. Easy conquest of the island was not expected, and when the Roman soldiers gathered along the shore of the mainland they paused, intimidated by what they saw. A report by Tacitus stated that,

> An opposing battle-line, thick with men and weapons, women rushing between them, like Furies in their funeral clothes, their hair flowing, carrying torches; Druids among them, pouring out frightful curses with their hands raised to high heaven, and pouring down frightful imprecations.

At last, encouraged by their leaders and standard bearers carrying the insignia of the imperial golden eagle, they swarmed across the Strait. The ensuing battle was long, hard and bloody. Describing what took place afterwards Tacitus continues,

> After the battle they placed garrisons in the towns, and cut down the groves consecrated to the most horrible superstitions; for the British held it right to sacrifice on their altars with the blood of their captives, and to consult the gods by the inspection of human entrails.

The Druids and the natives of ancient Mona were a thoroughly cruel lot, but the Romans, who also paid homage to pagan gods, were little better and just as cruel.

There is no need to wet your feet in crossing the Strait today, for 100ft above the water you can drive over the fine suspension bridge designed by Telford, and there is no opposition when you reach the end of the bridge. Below Telford's bridge another, carrying the railway spans the Strait; it was originally of tubular construction, but after being damaged by fire in 1970 the rails now run over a flat-arched girder bridge, then through Anglesey for twenty miles to Holyhead. For the motorist the A5 trunk highway, also engineered by Telford, runs almost through the centre of the island, and the distance to Holyhead is four or five miles less.

The fine Menai Strait Bridge, one of Telford's greatest achievements, carries the A55 London to Holyhead road across the Menai Strait to the island of Anglesey. Work started on the bridge in 1819, and it was the first bridge of its type in the world. In the museum at Bangor is a display of drawings which Telford prepared when designing the bridge

The A5 road passes through the market town of Llangefni, the administrative centre of Anglesey and also a good base for touring the island. Not far to the east of Llangefni is a small farmhouse which played an important role in the history of Britain. Plas Penmynydd was once the home of Owen Tudor who married the young widow of King Henry V. One of their three sons, Edmund, married the daughter of John of Gaunt, and they became the parents of Henry VII, the first Tudor King of England.

After crossing from the mainland, Menai Bridge is the first town you will reach in Anglesey. From there a coastal road runs for five miles to Beaumaris, the starting place of a route planned to keep as near to the coast as possible. King Edward I, 'the castle builder', felt that a fort at Beaumaris, together with that at Caernarfon, would hold down the Welsh and at the same time command the traffic sailing through the narrow Strait. Construction of the fortress commenced in 1295, and after three years' concentrated effort the first stage of the building was large enough to contain a garrison to guard the entry from the sea to the Menai Strait. With formidable towers evenly spaced along the perimeter wall it was obviously a very difficult castle to capture. Probably for this reason, and because there was more than enough territory on the mainland for the Welsh and Normans to squabble over, its history was comparatively uneventful. Consequently the building is in an exceptionally good state, and is one of the finest examples of an Edwardian concentric castle.

There are other places of interest: in Castle Street is a fifteenth-century house known as Tudor Rose, now used as an antique shop and art gallery; in Steeple Street is the gaol where you can see an old wooden treadmill and the place of execution. An ancient relic of the past is in the porch of Beaumaris Church in the shape of a coffin lid with an inscribed effigy said to be of the daughter of King John. The coffin, serving as a farm water-trough, was found in the nineteenth century. The sepulchre of the princess was originally in Llanfaes Priory. How the faithless wife of Prince Llywelyn Fawr, after her torrid affair with de Braose, came to be interred in the priory is not clear, but as a royal personage the honour of a marked tomb was due to her.

North of Beaumaris is Penmon which has a ruined priory, a wishing well and the remains of a primitive fort. The priory, founded by St Seriol in the sixth century, shows traces of Saxon work. Offshore is Puffin Island, a breeding place for the bird of that name. When the Danes landed on the island in about AD 853 and destroyed a monastic settlement they gave it the appropriate name of Priestholm. It was used as a burial place for the monks of Penmon Priory, and in AD 547 Madgwyn, King of Gwynedd, was buried there. He could not have been a very popular ruler for Gildus to describe him as

> Thou island dragon, first in wickedness, exceeding others in power and malice . . . prompt in sin.

Nearby are the ruins of Llanfaes Priory, the original burial place of Joan, daughter of King John and the erring wife of Llywelyn Fawr.

North of Beaumaris a complexity of lanes will bring you to a hill above the coast where are banks and ditches of an ancient fortification, marked on the map as Bwrdd Arthur. The local people are sure that it was here that King Arthur set up his Round Table. The hill fort overlooks Red Wharf Bay, a favourite landing place of Irish and Danish marauders, but a later landing is better remembered by the folk who live in this part of Anglesey. These unwelcome red-haired visitors formed a settlement on the land above the bay, and became widely known for their practice of witchcraft, but their place of origin remained a mystery.

From the small hamlet of Red Wharf a lane joins the main A5025 road to Benllech and Moelfre, two popular resorts with stretches of firm sands. Moelfre has a lifeboat station, a reminder of a night in October 1859 when an Australian ship bound for Liverpool was wrecked within sight of the beach, and 465 people were drowned. The cargo of this unfortunate ship, the *Royal Charter*, was gold to the value of £350,000. There is a ghoulish story that many of the drowned people washed ashore wore belts with pouches filled with nuggets of gold, and that the finding of this treasure enriched many of the local people. At this time the coast was unobserved, so although the wreck occurred close to the shore it was not known until daybreak. At Llanallgo churchyard stands an obelisk memorial to those drowned on the night of 15/16 October 1859. A neighbouring beach, Traeth Bychan, is associated with the tragedy of the submarine HMS *Thetis*, which failed to surface from trials in

1939 trapping ninety-nine men. It was later beached at Traeth Bychan.

Between Penysarn and Parys Mountain the road goes to Amlwch. When the copper-mining industry was busy during the eighteenth century Amlwch claimed to be the world's most important port for handling the copper mined from Parys Mountain. The small harbour is said to have handled more than eighty thousand tons of copper every year. The mines had their own currency and Amlwch Pennies are still unearthed occasionally. The Romans are said to have made use of the copper from Parys Mountain, and the remains of a Roman bathhouse near Amlwch confirm that they knew this little port on the north coast of Anglesey.

As well as bringing prosperity to Amlwch through trade, the busy port was responsible for admitting the plague. This happened when the bodies of some seamen, thrown overboard after death from the plague were washed up in Bull Bay. One of them still wore a red cap; this was fancied by a villager who took it from the corpse. Within a few days of wearing it he was infected with the disease which became known as the 'Plague of the Red Cap', a plague that spread through the surrounding area.

Amlwch once had a thriving tobacco-processing industry, Amlwch Shag being widely known among pipe smokers. There was also a substantial boat-building industry run by the Treweek family, this latter industry continuing into the 1930s.

From Amlwch port a lane runs to the edge of the cliff at Point Lynas and Llaneilian Church. The latter is one of the most interesting in Anglesey; dedicated to St Eilian it dates from the twelfth century. Inside is a rood screen with some unusual decoration, and even more unusual is the saint's chapel which you can only enter by squeezing through a narrow passage. However, if this has been difficult you can be compensated for your effort, for by turning round three times you will be cured of any ailment. At least this is different from the usual cure obtained by drinking well-water—but there is a choice, for if you have more faith in wells the saint provided one near the church. Ffynnon Eilian is multi-purpose, to be used for healing, wishing and cursing. For the latter purpose you need to bore a hole in a piece of slate, insert in it a wax figure of the person you wish to discomfort—then after writing his name on the slate, attach it to a piece of cork and drop it in the well. As long as the slate stays submerged in the well the person you dislike will suffer bad health.

Between Bull Bay and Cemaes Bay the coast becomes rockier, the cliffs higher and the sea currents treacherous. Cemaes is distinguished by having the only ancient church in Wales dedicated to St Patrick. It was somewhere nearby that the Irish saint landed after a miraculous voyage across the Irish Sea in 'a coracle propelled without oars or sail'. His name is also perpetuated by a small offshore island called Ynys Badrig, 'the Island of Patrick'. From Cemaes the general direction of the road (the A5025) is southwards until it joins the A5 trunk road through Anglesey at Valley where one of the richest finds of the prehistoric age in Wales was unearthed.

From Valley an embankment carries road and railway across the Beddmanarch Bay into Holy Island, road and railway ending at Holyhead from where you can take a ship to Dublin. As a port of embarkation it is a busy place, but in less than half an hour you can reach Stack Point where there is fine cliff scenery and above the Point is the summit of Holyhead Mountain. The view from the summit embraces the Irish coast, Snowdonia, the Isle of Man and the dim-blue mountains of the Lake District peaks. On the lower slope of the mountain is the fort of Gaer-y-Twr, and there are other high places with ancient stones giving certain evidence of early occupation.

Five miles along the A5 southeastwards from Valley a right-hand turn, the A4080, runs through Llanfaelog to Aberffraw where the princes of North Wales built their palaces. There is little left today to remind the tourist of the past historical importance of this pleasant village. If history has not been affected by the embroidery of legend the next village of Llangadwaladr is of even greater importance. Its name certainly supports the claim that it was once the home of a British noble who insisted that he was the true king of all Britain. There can be no doubt that the family who lived here centuries ago were respected for their wisdom and quality of leadership, for an inscribed gravestone is accepted as being that of King Cadwalladr's grandfather. It has a Latin inscription telling us that he was 'CATAMANUS, wisest and most illustrious of all Kings'.

After crossing the Afon Cefni where it finds an outlet into the

Malltraeth Sands, a large inlet of marsh and sand, there is Newborough, a village with an Anglo-Saxon-sounding name, but in the reign of Edward I it was called Rhosyr. From the village a lane crosses Newborough Warren to a narrow neck of land where, before sinking beneath the sand dunes, traces of a fifth-century monastic building could be seen. It was here that several important Welsh squires and soldiers are supposed to have met in secret to start the events which brought Henry Tudor from exile in France to fight for the establishment of the royal Tudor lineage.

Between Newborough and Menai Bridge there are other interesting places. On the shore of the Menai Strait is Llidan Church where the bowl of a holy water stoup never needed refilling. Giraldus, who loved a fanciful story, writes of a stone cemented in the wall of the church which was shaped like a thigh bone. According to Giraldus, 'whatever distance it is carried it returns of its own accord'. Near Llanddaniel is Bryn Celli Ddu, accepted as being the finest example of a prehistoric burial chamber in Wales, and in nearby woods are groves which are said to have once been revered as sacred by the Druids.

Before ending this Anglesey journey a visit should be made to Plas Newydd, a fine eighteenth-century mansion given by the Marquess of Anglesey to the National Trust, and open to the public since 1976. The present house is 'new' but its history commenced five hundred years ago. The gardens stretching along the shoreline of the Menai Strait are very beautiful. Ask any Englishman, or a non-Welsh speaking native of North Wales, where Plas Newydd is situated and he will most likely say 'at Menai Bridge'. If he does attempt to give a more definite point of location he will say 'at Llanfair P.G.' For him to give the place its full name is something of a tongue-twister, but it is musical, poetical and descriptive—so take a deep breath and try: Llanfairpwllgwyngyllgogerychwyrndrobwllllandysiliogogogoch. With typical Welsh logic in place-names which are almost a local guide, it means 'Church of St Mary in a hollow of white hazel, near to a rapid whirlpool and to St Tysilio's church, near to a red cave'. What place, with this Welsh name-poetry singing through the brain, could be a better one to conclude a journey round the fair isle of Mona?

From Porthmadog the obvious tourist route to explore the peninsula is signposted to Criccieth. Sheltered from the cold northern winds by the mountains of Snowdonia Criccieth enjoys a climate which is remarkably mild throughout the year. After the turbulent past when Romans and then Normans battled against the Welsh this is now a peaceful seaside resort, one of the most popular in North Wales.

Aware of its importance as a strategic position the Welsh built a castle here many years before the Normans came, but when Edward I forded the Afon Glaslyn he, too, appreciated the military possibilities of the Welsh fortress, so it was not long before he attacked and won the castle. Over the years it was the scene of many battles, some so fierce that in places the stonework has been split by the heat from fire.

King Edward I, anxious to make a quick penetration further into North Wales, left a permanent garrison to hold the castle for him. One of the castle wardens was known as Sir Hywel of the Poleaxe, so named because he used this weapon with such devastating effect at the Battle of Poitiers. There may be some foundation in this story, but little in the one that during the course of the battle he captured the French king. Glyndwr, living up to his reputation, raged through the town on his way to assault Caernarfon Castle, but even he failed to take Criccieth. Ask anyone today what the name of Criccieth means to them; they will not connect it with the name of an English king or with Owain Glyndwr, but will remember that the greatest Welshman of his time spent his boyhood here, and is buried a short way out of the town.

The poor lad, who became Prime Minister of the United Kingdom, was brought up by his uncle, Richard Lloyd, a local shoemaker. When you reach Llanystumdwy, just outside Criccieth, ask in any of the local inns which is the house where young David Lloyd George spent his early years and you will be given unfailing directions on how to find the small cottage of Richard Lloyd. So proud were the local people of David that after his death they arranged to house many of his personal possessions in a memorial museum, just a short way from his cottage home. He was buried at Llanystumdwy; the stream along which he often walked and his simple grave attract many summer visitors.

This part of North Wales became even more popular after Sir

Billy Butlin built a large holiday camp about four miles or so along the coast. Beyond the camp is Pwllheli, a market town which was granted a charter by the Black Prince in 1355. As a seaside resort its attractions are obvious, and the climate is as moderate as at Criccieth. If you wish to holiday at a quieter resort carry on to Llanbedrog where you will find less crowded beaches and sheltered coves. The headland of Mynydd Trwyn Llanbedrog projects into Cardigan Bay, and from it there are extensive views. To the south is the bay of St Tudwal with its twin islands, and for the painter and photographer the village presents many picturesque subjects for brush and camera. North of the Llanbedrog—Abersoch road is a Jacobean manor, Castellmarch, reputed to be the site of a castle belonging to a king called March, who had horse's ears. To keep this fact a secret he killed every barber who trimmed his hair.

Abersoch rivals Llanbedrog as an attractive place to spend a holiday. Three miles offshore are St Tudwal's Islands—the east one has the remains of a twelfth-century chapel, and the west island has a lighthouse. A mile west of Abersoch, at Llanengan, is a church considered to be the most interesting one on the peninsula. This sanctuary was founded centuries before St Tudwal sailed across the bay to build a chapel on his island site. Inside there is a beautiful rood screen, also ceremonial plate and vessels from the abbey which once stood on Bardsey Island. There is also a memorial stone a hundred years older than the church in honour of Melus, the doctor son of Martinus. This is the first known mention of a doctor in Wales.

Llanengan must be one of the peninsula's most exposed villages, for only a short distance away is the six-mile-wide bay of Porth Nicgwl—'Hell's Mouth', an apt name for it is open to the full force of the south-westerly gales. It is an inhospitable stretch of coast backed by an almost vertical buttress of high cliffs. The bay curves round to the headland of Trwyn Talfarach with a foreshore and cliffs which are almost as savage, but when the western headland is rounded there are compensations to be found in the Bay of Aberdaron.

Aberdaron has several distinctions; it is the most remote village in the peninsula, and is also on the 'pilgrim way' to the island of Bardsey. Visitors to the village can have their 'elevenses' and buy souvenirs in Y Gegin Fawr, 'the Big Kitchen', sitting on the very spot where the pilgrims to Bardsey refreshed themselves before embarking on the rough sea crossing to the holy island.

A few miles away is the tip of the peninsula which has rightly been named 'the Land's End of Wales'. Near the edge of the cliffs the outline of St Mary's Church can still be seen. It was the last church on the mainland where the pilgrims could stop and pray to God for a safe crossing of the Bardsey Sound. It does not require much imagination to picture the scene in the little church. The ill-clad pilgrims, weary and footsore, crowding the dim rush-lit sanctuary attending a mass, with the officiating priest blessing them, offering prayers for their safe journey across the sea on the following morning. The island of Bardsey was considered to be a holy place, and to make a pilgrimage there was just as important for spiritual benefit as a journey to the shrine of St David's in Pembrokeshire. Three journeys to Bardsey were considered equal to making one to St Peter's in Rome; two journeys were required to St David's.

There is very little left of the early sixth-century abbey which St Cadfan founded on the island. Six or seven years after it was built Drubicius, Archbishop of Wales, retired there, but when he died his body was eventually removed to Llandaff in South Wales. In AD 603 the Saxons raided and sacked the abbey at Bangor Iscoed, causing the monks to seek peace and refuge at Bardsey, so it was soon held to be a safe haven for the inmates of other monasteries. This may account for the island being called 'the Isle of Saints', for it is claimed that as many as 20,000 holy men were buried there.

From Aberdaron the road (B4413/B4417) runs back along the northern side of the peninsula through Tudweiliog to Morfa Nefyn, an excellent centre for the walker and a convenient one for climbing the Rivals, the highest group of peaks in the Lleyn Peninsula. There are no traces of an ancient church or castle at Nefyn, but the village has memories of the past. Some nearby fields were used in 1284 by Edward I when he held a tournament to celebrate, although some thought it premature, his conquest of Wales. Champions came from England and the continent to compete in contests of military skill. Morfa Nefyn had its port at Dinllaen, a place busy with coastal trade and embarkation for ships to Ireland and trading ports along Cardigan Bay. From the west end of Porth Dinllaen a narrow headland juts out into Caernarfon Bay, supporting a lifeboat station and the remains of a cliff castle.

The B4417 road out of Nefyn is marked on the map as 'Saints Road to Bardsey'. When Llithfaen is reached a lane leads to a point from where Yr Eifl, one of the three peaks of the Rivals, can be climbed. Two miles away, at Llanaelhaearn, the pilgrim's road joins the A499 trunk road—a convenient point for climbing the other two Rival peaks. The summit of one of these peaks is crowned with what was once the most important prehistoric town in North Wales, with stone walls probably enclosing a hundred or more hut circles. This peak, Tre'r Ceiri—'the Giants' Town'—is named after the settlement whose walls still rise in parts, to a height of 15ft and enclosed an area of five acres. When the Romans came they added further fortifications and used it as a strongpoint. Between these mountains and the sea Vortigern is supposed to have had a castle; the exact site is uncertain, but when a tumulus reported to be his burial place was excavated the bones of a very tall man were found.

At the northern foot of the Rivals is Clynnog-fawr where two ancient pilgrim routes met. The village is very attractive, and the church of St Beuno contains much to interest the historian and the architectural student. The square proportions of the chancel are unusual; the rood screen is very fine; and some of the misereri seats of the stalls are imaginatively carved with human heads wearing a variety of strange headgear. Fixed on the wall is a relic of the days when dogs found their way into the church. This is a 'lazy-tong' which extended to enable the warden to capture and eject the unwelcome canine visitor.

St Beuno was much concerned for the good health of his parishioners, so he left by the roadside a well where they could cleanse themselves before spending a night kneeling in prayer on the saint's altar tomb within the old chapel. After this they were miraculously cured of practically any affliction.

From Clynnog-fawr and the Rivals the long straight road runs for six miles to Llanwnda where it divides, the right-hand branch going south across the head of the peninsula back to Porthmadog, the starting place of this tour. The continuation of the road from Clynnog-fawr heads north to reach Caernarfon.

Glossary of Welsh Words

Aber	river mouth, confluence	Cleddau	swords
		Clogwyn	precipice
Afon	river	Clwyd	gate
Allt	hill-side	Cob	embankment
Ap	son of	Coch	red
Bach	small (feminine: fach)	Coed	wood
		Craig	rock, crag (mutated form: y graig)
Bardd	bard, poet		
Bedd	grave	Crib	comb, a narrow ridge
Betws	chapel		
Blaen	upper reaches of valley or river	Croes	cross (mutated form: y groes)
Brân	crow	Crug	mound
Bras	rich, large	Cwm	valley
Brenin	king	Cymro	Welshman
Bron	breast of a hill	Da	good
Bryn	hill	Dan	under
Bwlch	pass	Dau	two
Cadair, cader	chair	Dewi	David
		Dinas	fort, city
Cae	field	Dôl	meadow
Caer	fort (mutated form: y gaer)	Drws	door
		Du, ddu	black
Calch	lime	Dwr	water
Cant	one hundred	Dyffryn	valley
Cantref	division of land	Eglwys	church
Capel	chapel	Esgair	hill, spur
Carn, carnedd	cairn	Ffordd	road
		Ffos	ditch
Carreg	stone	Ffridd	mountain pasture
Castell	castle	Garth	hill, ridge
Cefn	back, ridge	Ger	near, by
Ceiliog	lock	Glan	clean
Ceunant	ravine	Glas	green, blue
Cil	recess, retreat	Glyn	glen, valley
Cistfaen	prehistoric grave	Gorsaf	station
Clawdd	dyke, embankment	Gwasted	plain, flat

Glossary of Welsh Words

Gwaun	meadow	*Pant*	valley, hollow
Gwely	bed	*Parc*	park
Gwern	swamp, alder-trees	*Pen*	top, head
Gwig	wood	*Pentref*	village
Hafod	summer dwelling	*Pistyll*	waterfall
Helyg	willows	*Plas*	mansion
Hendre	winter dwelling	*Pont*	bridge
Heol	road	*Porth*	port
Hir	long	*Pump*	five
Hiraeth	yearning	*Pwll*	pool
Hwyl	mood, inspiration	*Rhiw*	hill
Isaf	lowest	*Rhos*	moor, plain
Llan	enclosure, church	*Rhyd*	ford
Llech	slate	*Saesneg*	English language
Llethr	slope	*Sant*	saint
Llwybr	path	*Sarn*	causeway
Llwyn	grove	*Sir*	county
Llyn	lake	*Sych*	dry
Llys	court	*Tad*	father
Mab	son	*Taren*	knoll, rock
Maen	stone	*Teg*	fair
Maes	field	*Tir*	land
Mam	mother	*Tomen*	mound
Mawn	peat	*Traeth*	beach
Mawr	big	*Traws*	across
Melin	mill	*Tre, tref*	town, home
Melyn	yellow	*Tri*	three
Min	edge, brink	*Trum*	ridge
Moch	pigs	*Twll*	hole
Moel	bare, rounded hill	*Ty*	house
Môr	sea	*Tylwyth,*	
Morfa	bog, sea-marsh	*teg*	the fairies
Mur	wall	*Uchaf*	highest
Mynach	monk	*Uwch*	higher
Mynydd	mountain	*Waen*	meadow
Nant	stream, brook	*Y*	the, of the
Neuadd	hall	*Yn*	in, at
Newydd	new	*Ynys*	island
Nos	night	*Ysbryd*	spirit, ghost
Oer	cold	*Ysbyty*	hospital
Ogof	cave	*Ysgol*	school
Olaf	last	*Ysgubor*	barn
Pandy	fulling-mill	*Ystrad*	vale

Further Reading

General Guide Books

Barrett, J. H. *The Pembrokeshire Coast Path* (HMSO, 1974, for Countryside Commission)

Betjeman, J. & Piper, J. *Shell Guide Book to Wales* (Faber)

Thomas, W. V. & Llewellyn, Alun *The Shell Guide to Wales* (Michael Joseph, 1969)

Wales Tourist Board *South Wales Guide*; *Mid-Wales Guide*; *North Wales Guide*; *Castles and Historic Places*; *Wales—A Glimpse of the Past*

Topographical

Barber, W. T. *West of the Wye* (R. H. Johns, 1965)

Barber, Chris *Exploring the Brecon Beacons National Park* (Regional Publications, 1980)

Borrow, George *Wild Wales* (Collins)

Bradley, A. G. *The March and Borderland of Wales* (Constable)

—— *Highways and Byways in North Wales* (Constable)

—— *Highways and Byways in South Wales* (Constable)

Condry, William *Exploring Wales* (Faber, 1970)

Gardner, Don *Exploring the heart of Wales by car* (Cambrian News, 1970)

—— *Discovering Mid-Wales* (John Jones, 1978)

Jones, P. T. *Welsh Border Country* (Batsford, 1938)

Lewis, Eilund & Peter *The Land of Wales* (Batsford, 1937)

Lloyd, E. M. & D. M. *A Book of Wales* (Collins, 1953)

Massingham, H. J. *The Southern Marches* (Robert Hale, 1952)

Mais, S. P. B. *Highways & Byways in the Welsh Marches* (Macmillan, 1939)

Morton, H. V. *In Search of Wales* (Methuen, 1932)

North, F. J. *The river scenery at the head of the river Neath* (National Museum of Wales, 1949)

Palmer, W. T. *The Splendour of Wales* (Harrap, 1932)

Phillips, Olive *Monmouthshire* (Robert Hale, 1951)

—— *Gower* (Robert Hale, 1956)

Poucher, W. A. *The Welsh Peaks* (Constable, 1962)

Thomas, Ruth *South Wales* (Bartholomew, 1977)

Toulson, Shirley & Godwin, Fay *The Drovers' Roads of Wales* (Wildwood House, 1977)

Further Reading

Historical

Cox, William *An Historical Tour of Monmouthshire* (Dent)
Cambrensis, Giraldus *An Itinerary through Wales* 1188
Dodd, A. H. *A short history of Wales* (Batsford, 1972)
—— *Welsh life and customs*
Geoffrey of Monmouth *History of the Kings of Britain* (Dent)
Williams, David *History of Monmouthshire 1796*

Novels

Cordell, Alexander *Rape of the Fair Country* (Gollancz, 1959)
—— *The Hosts of Rebecca* (Gollancz, 1960)
—— *Song of the Earth* (Gollancz, 1969)
Firbank, Thomas *I bought a Mountain* (Harrap, 1940)
Gibbings, Robert *Coming down the Wye* (Dent, 1943)
Llewellyn, Richard *How Green was my Valley* (Michael Joseph, 1975)
Shipway, George *Imperial Governor* (Granada, 1970)
Smart, W. J. *Where Wye and Severn Flow*

Legends

Guest, Charlotte *The Mabinogion* (Dent)
Styles, Showell *Welsh Walks and Legends* (John Jones, 1972)
—— *Welsh Walks and Legends, South Wales* (John Jones, 1977)

Architecture and Archaeology

Boyle, N. E. *Old Parish Churches*
Boumphrey, G. M. *Along the Roman Roads* (Allen & Unwin, 1935)
Cottrell, C. *Seeing Roman Britain*
Fox, Sir Cyril *Ancient Monuments in South Wales and Monmouthshire*
  (HMSO, 1938)
—— *Life and Death in the Bronze Age* (Routledge & Kegan Paul, 1959)
Hawkes, J. and C. *Prehistoric Britain* (Penguin, 1958)
Hilling, J. B. *Historic Architecture of Wales* (University Press of Wales,
  1976)
Piggott, Stuart *Approach to Archaeology* (A&C Black, 1939)
Russell, A. L. N. *Architecture*
Thom, A. C. *Megalithic sites in Britain* (Oxford University Press, 1967)
Weigall, A. *Wanderings in Roman Britain*
Wheeler, Sir Mortimer *Prehistoric and Roman Wales*
Watkins, Alfred *The Old Straight Track* (Methuen, 1925; Garnstone
  Press, 1970)

Index

Index

Index